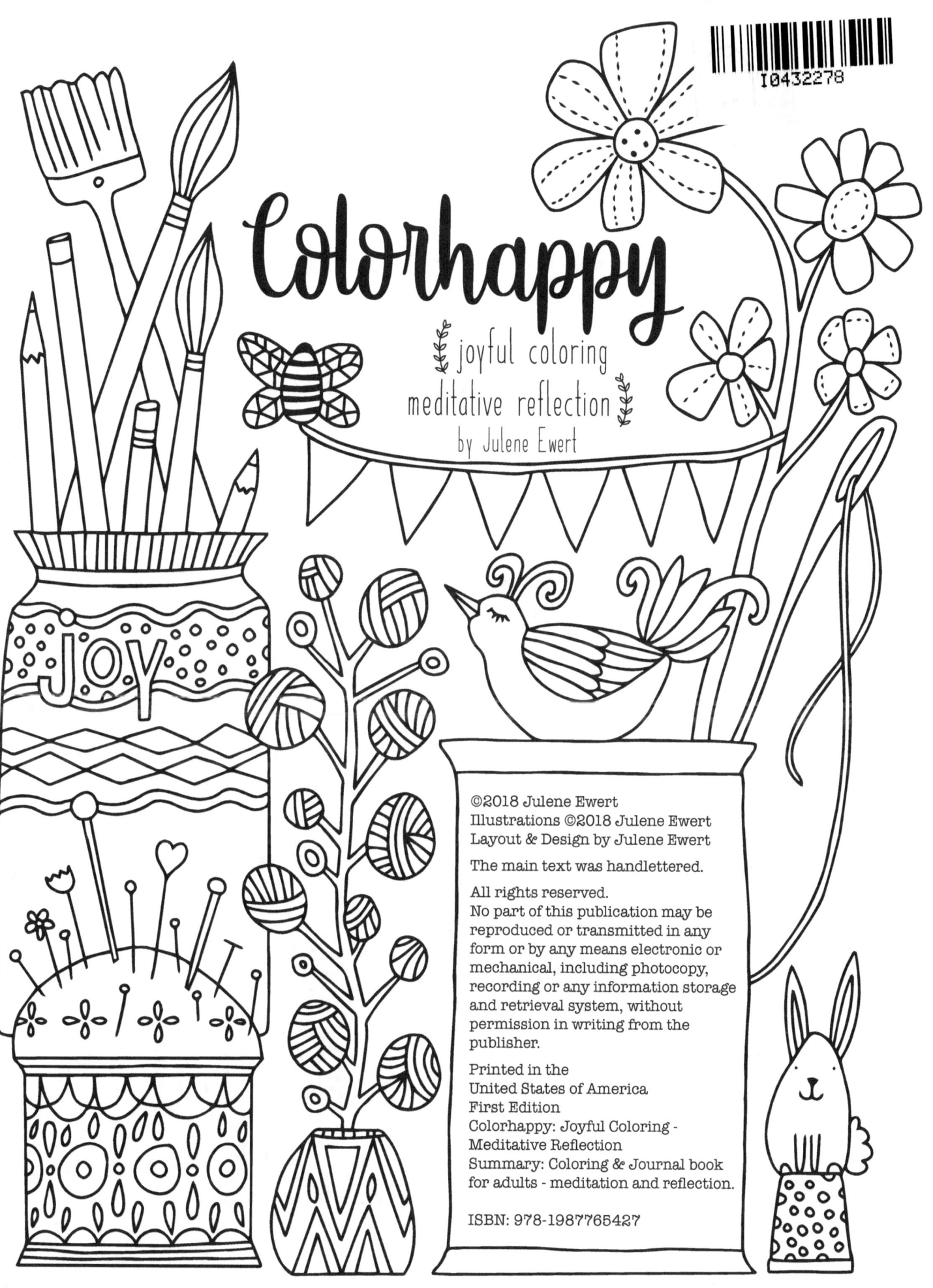

How do you Nourish your Soul...

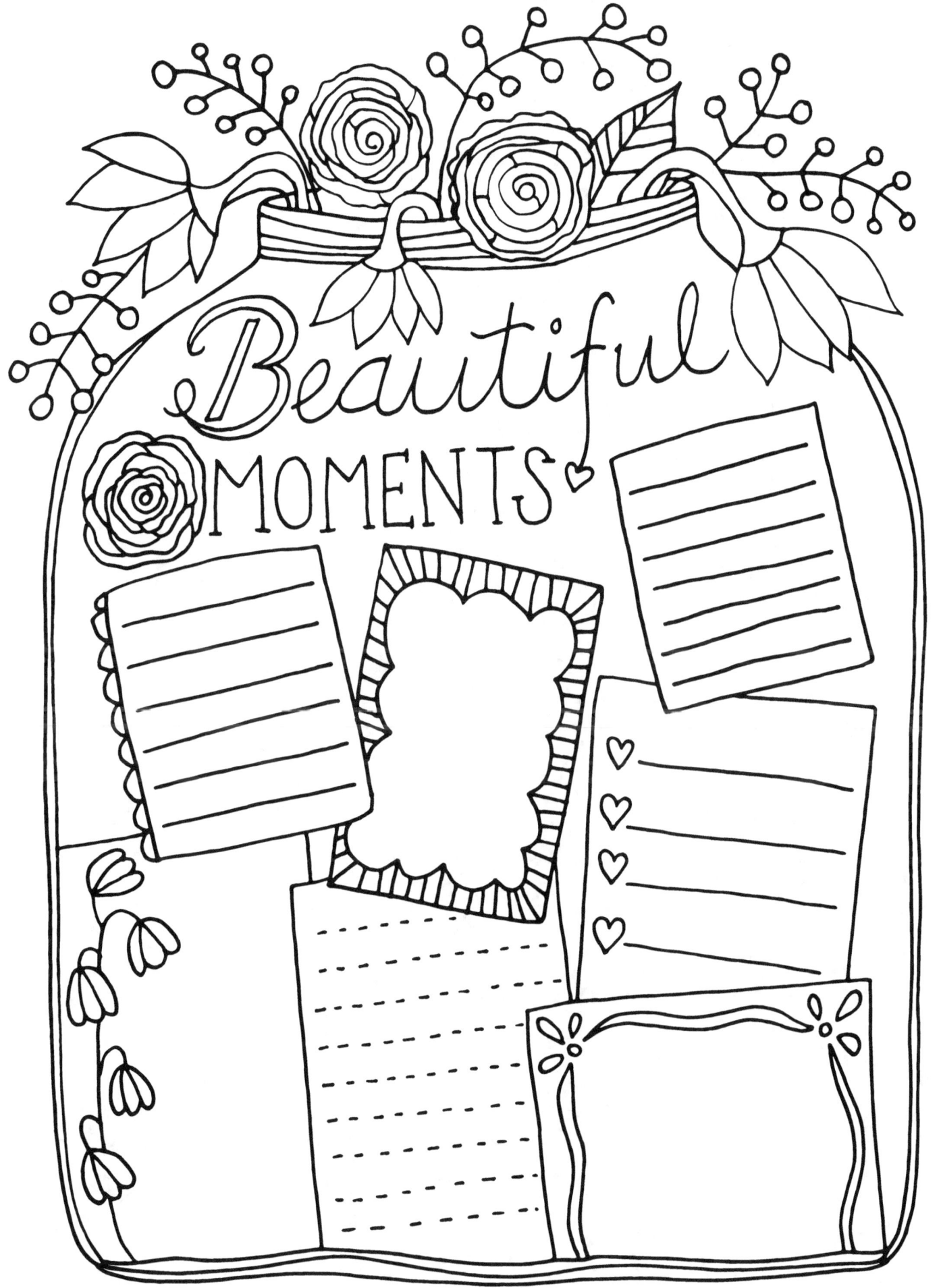

if you could change directions in your life...

❓ What would you do?

🌐 Where would you go?

☺ Who would you bring with you?

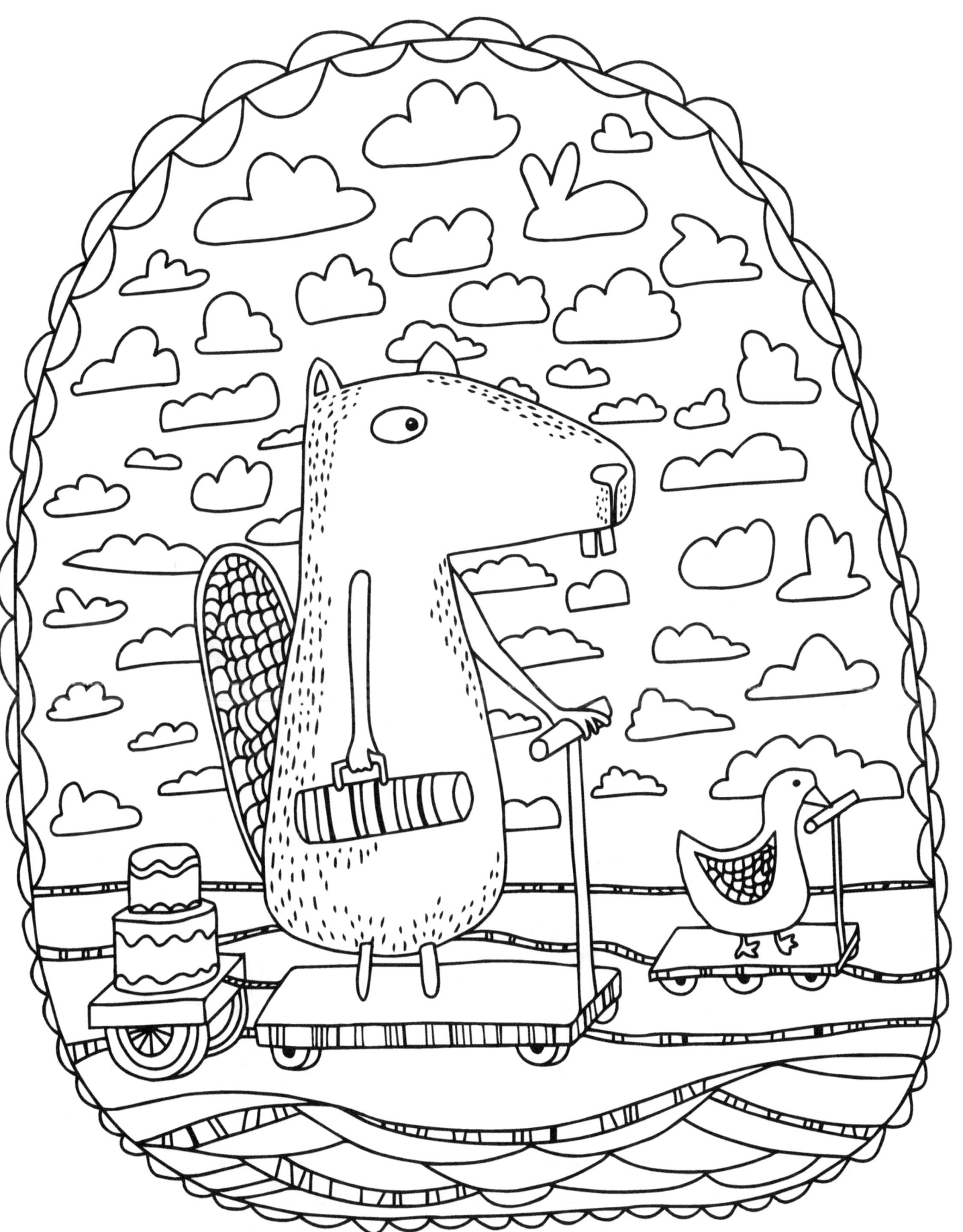

things that make me smile

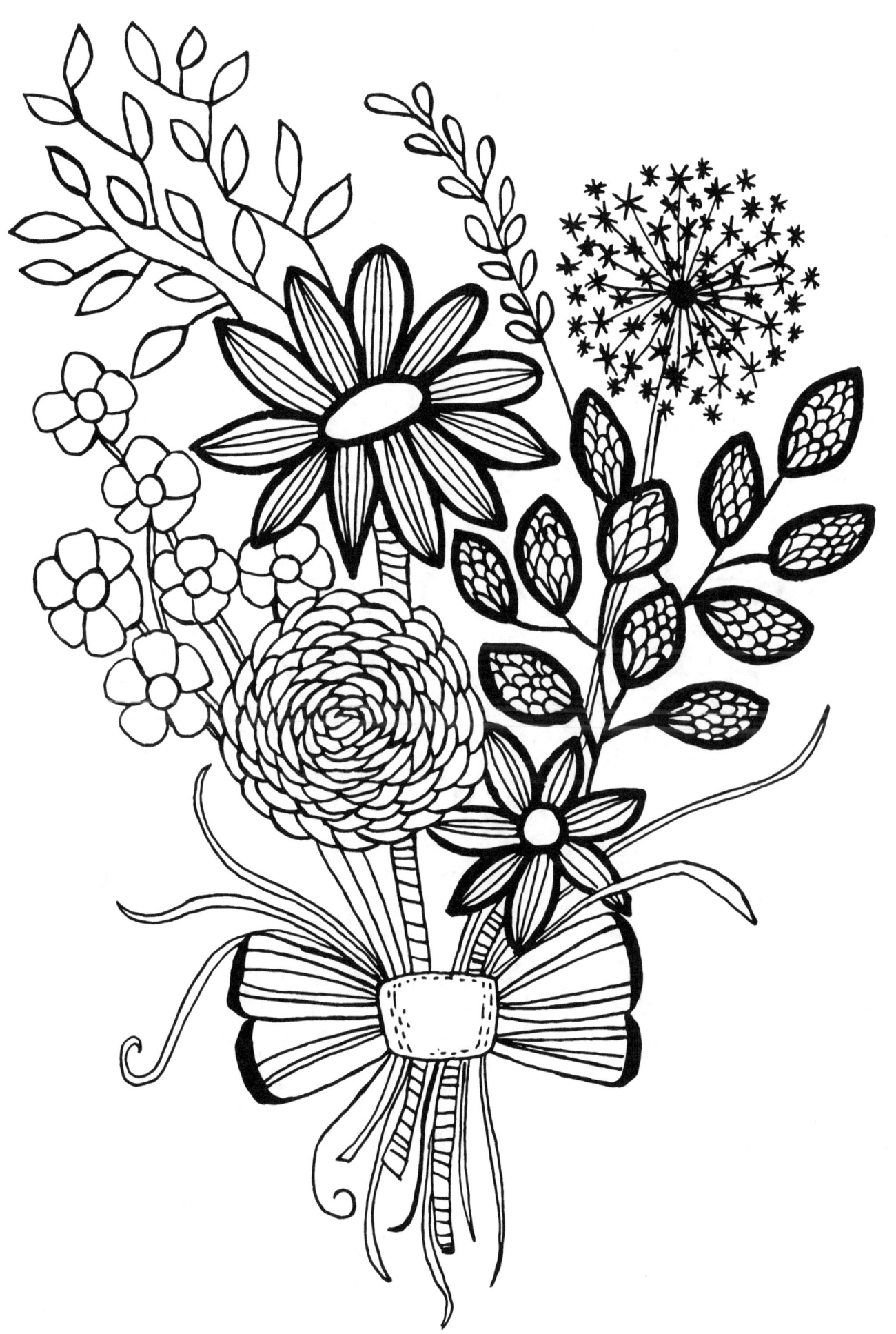

If you could
go back in time
and change
One thing
from your Past...
What would it be?

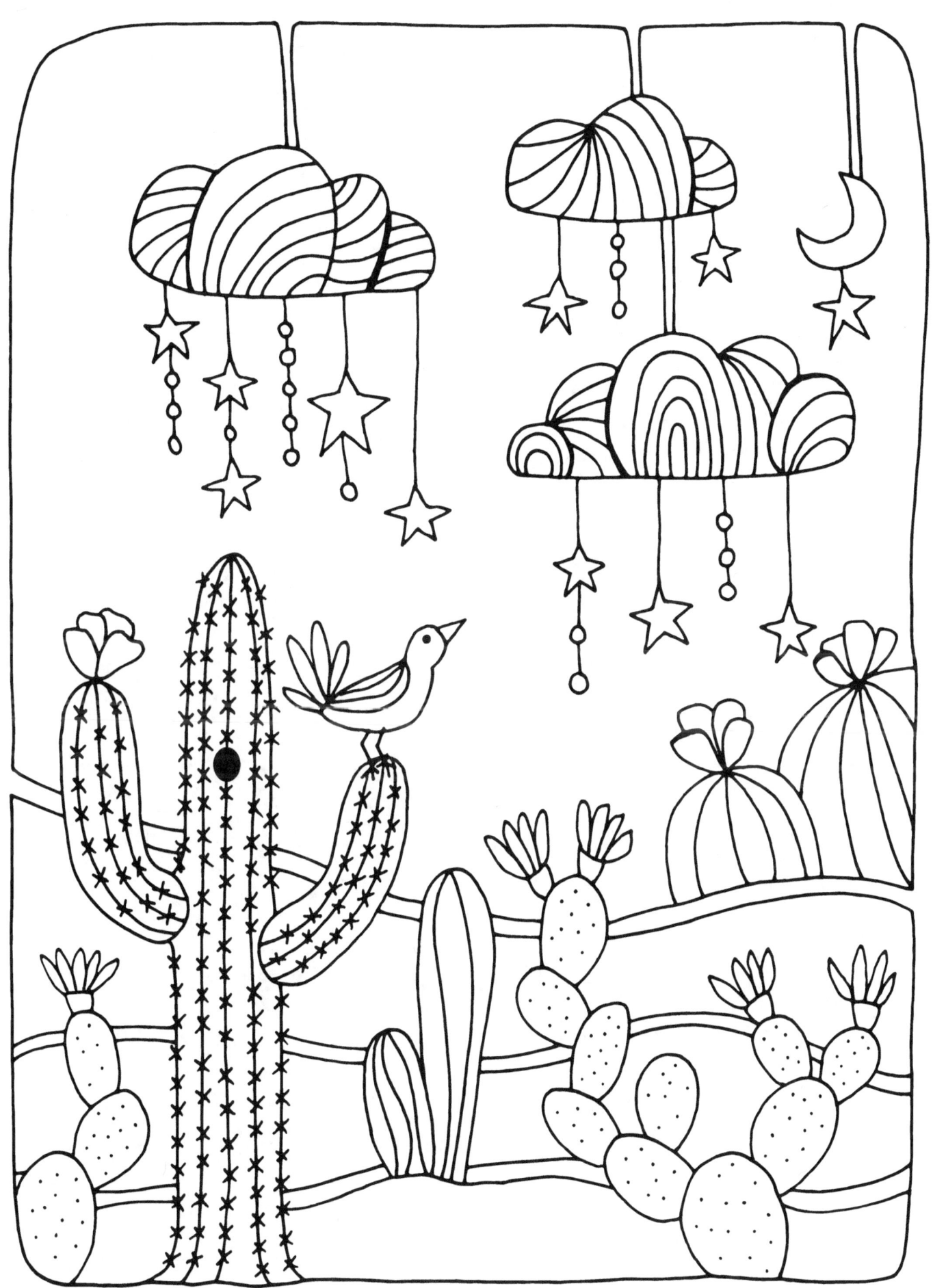

WHAT MAKES YOU *unique?*

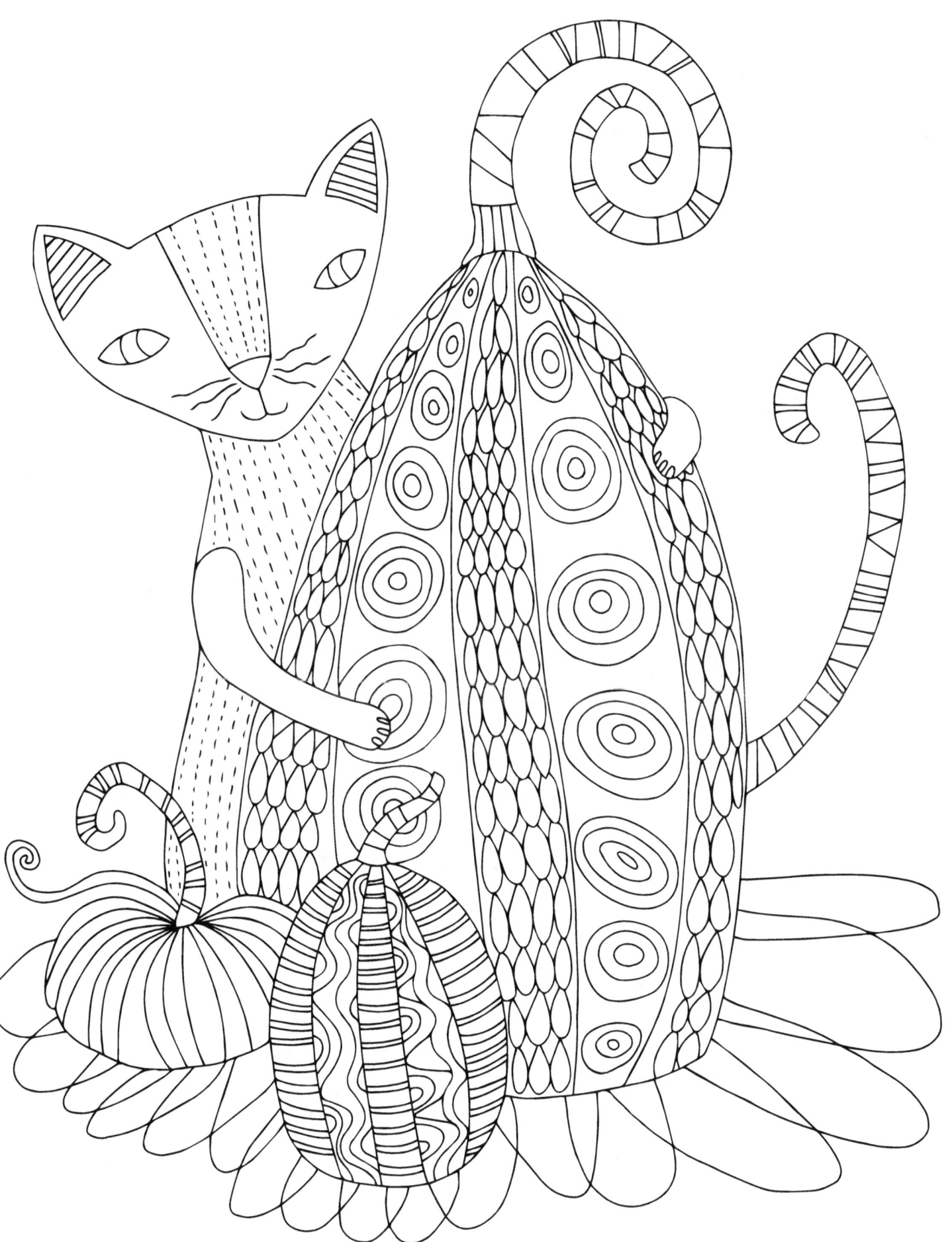

WHAT IS YOUR *Favorite* SEASON? Why?

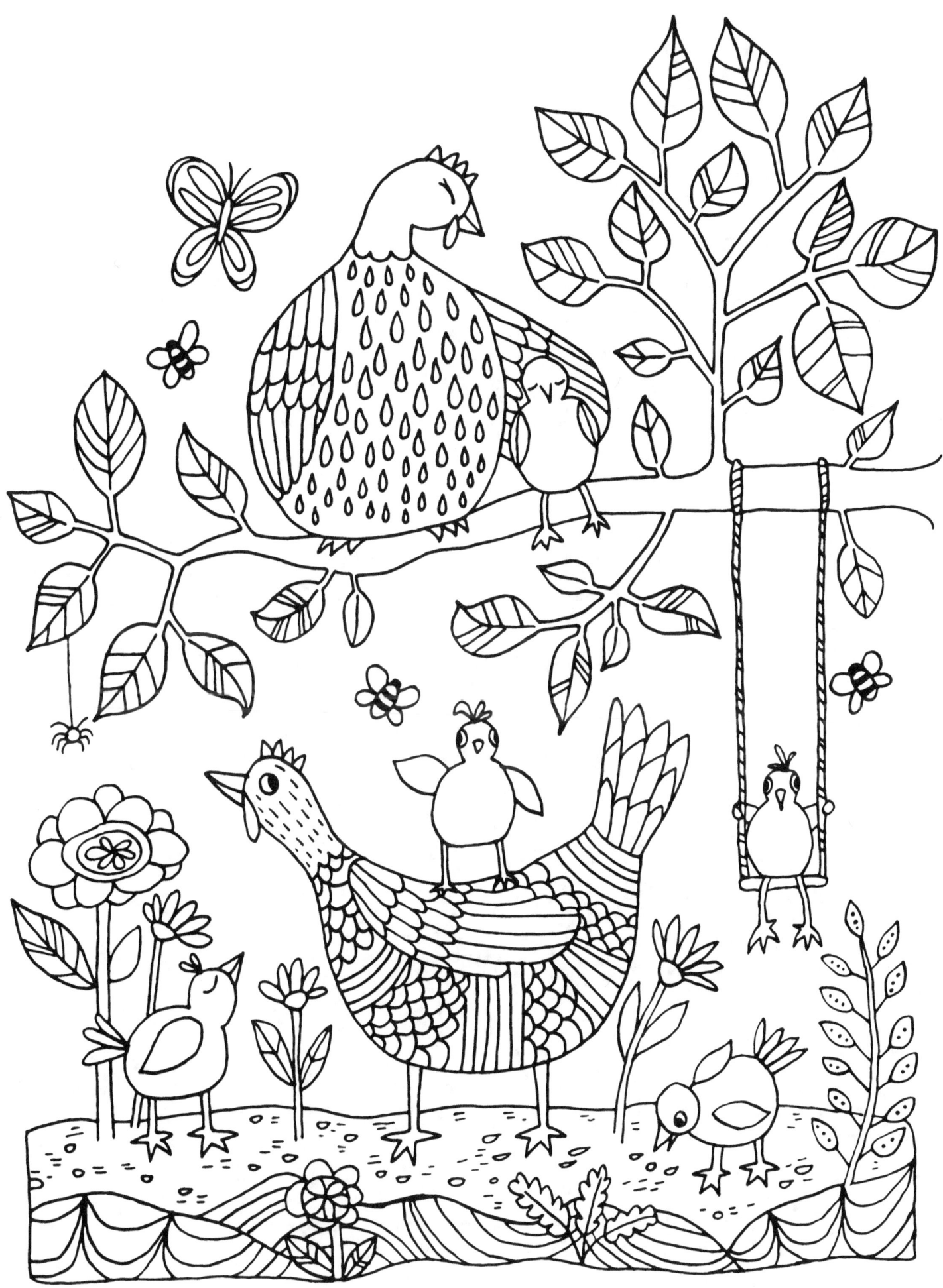

how do you focus?

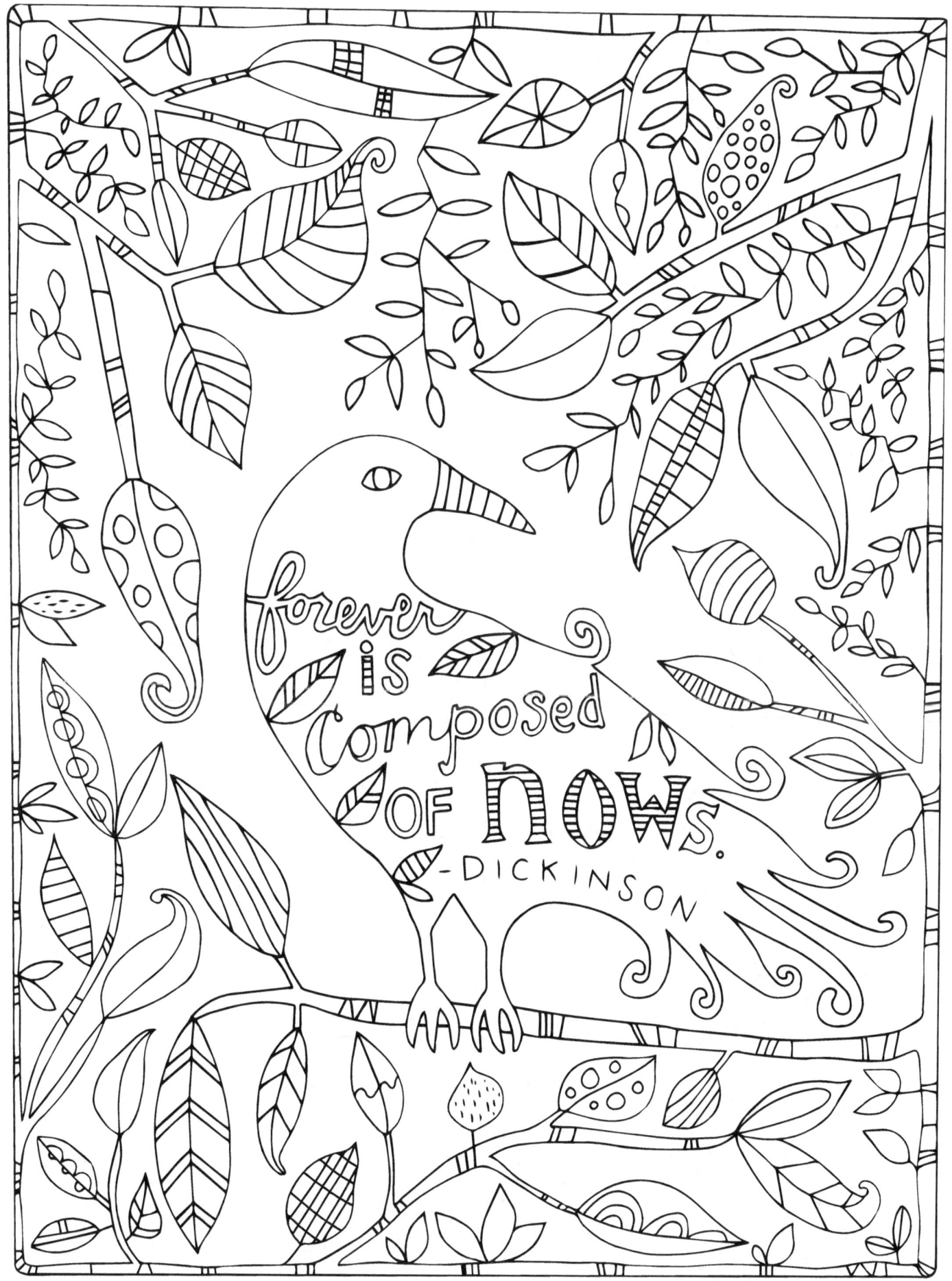

what is your greatest Strength?

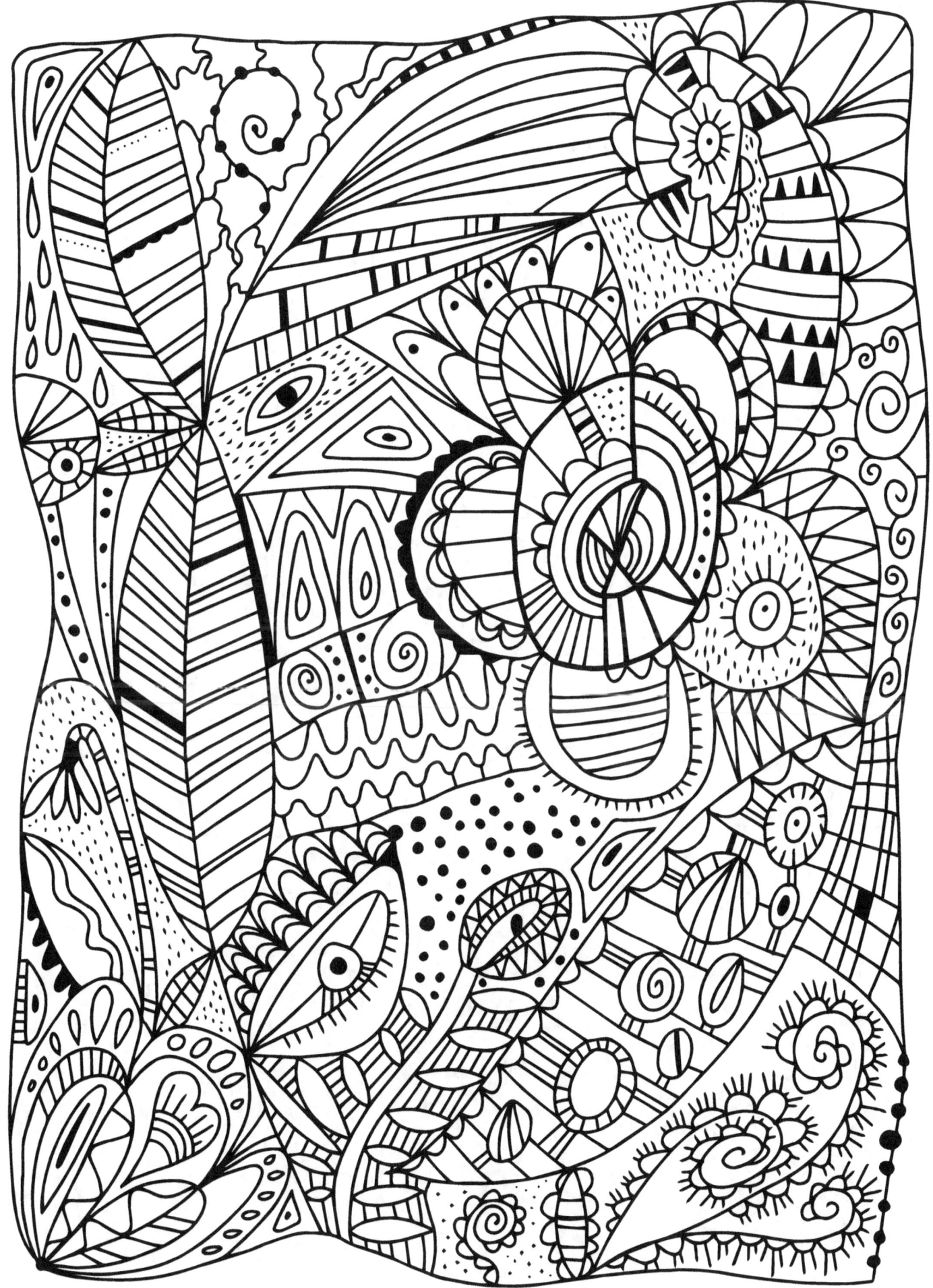

a List of places YOU have visited...

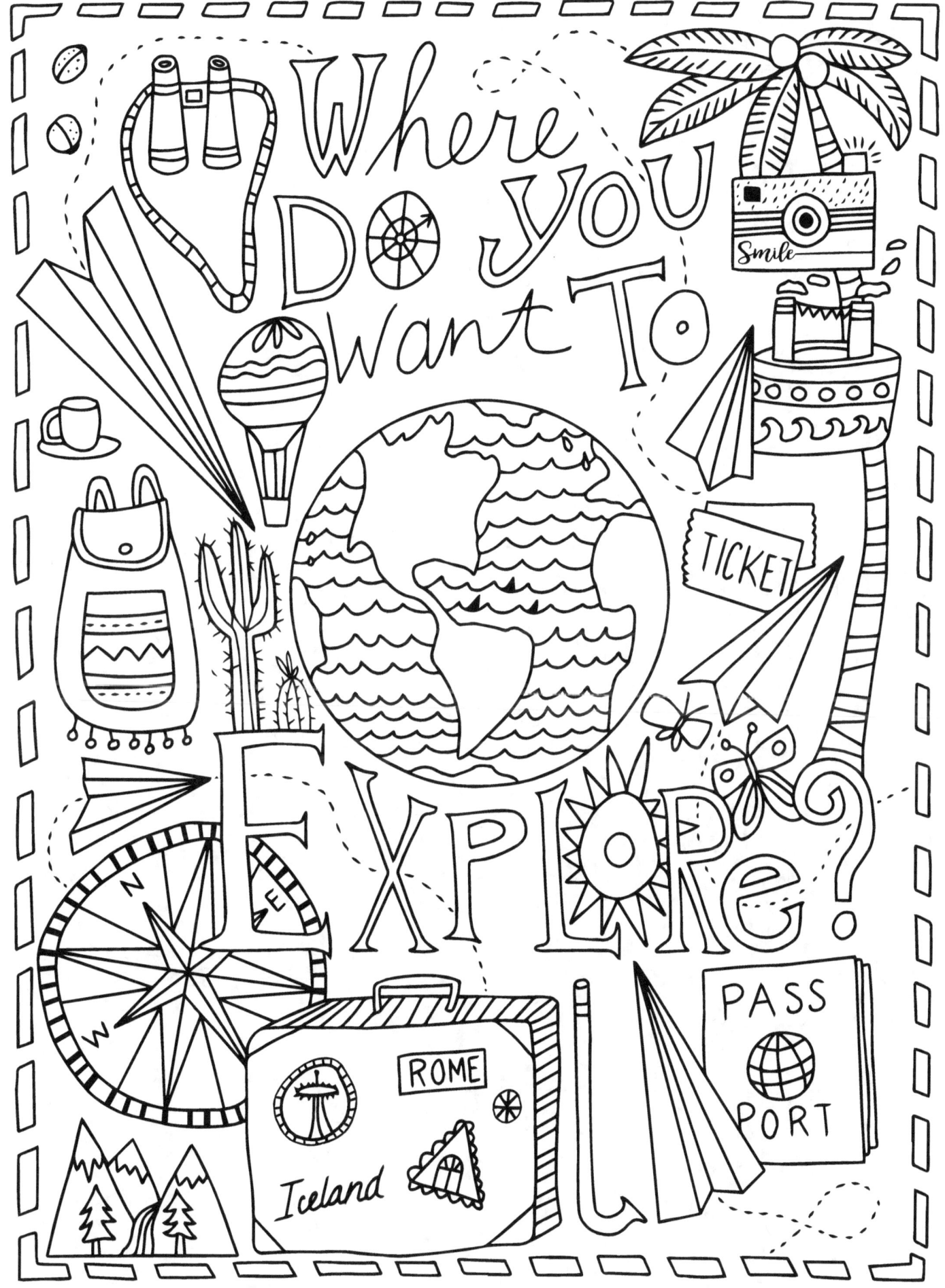

if you could become an expert in any subject or activity what would it be?

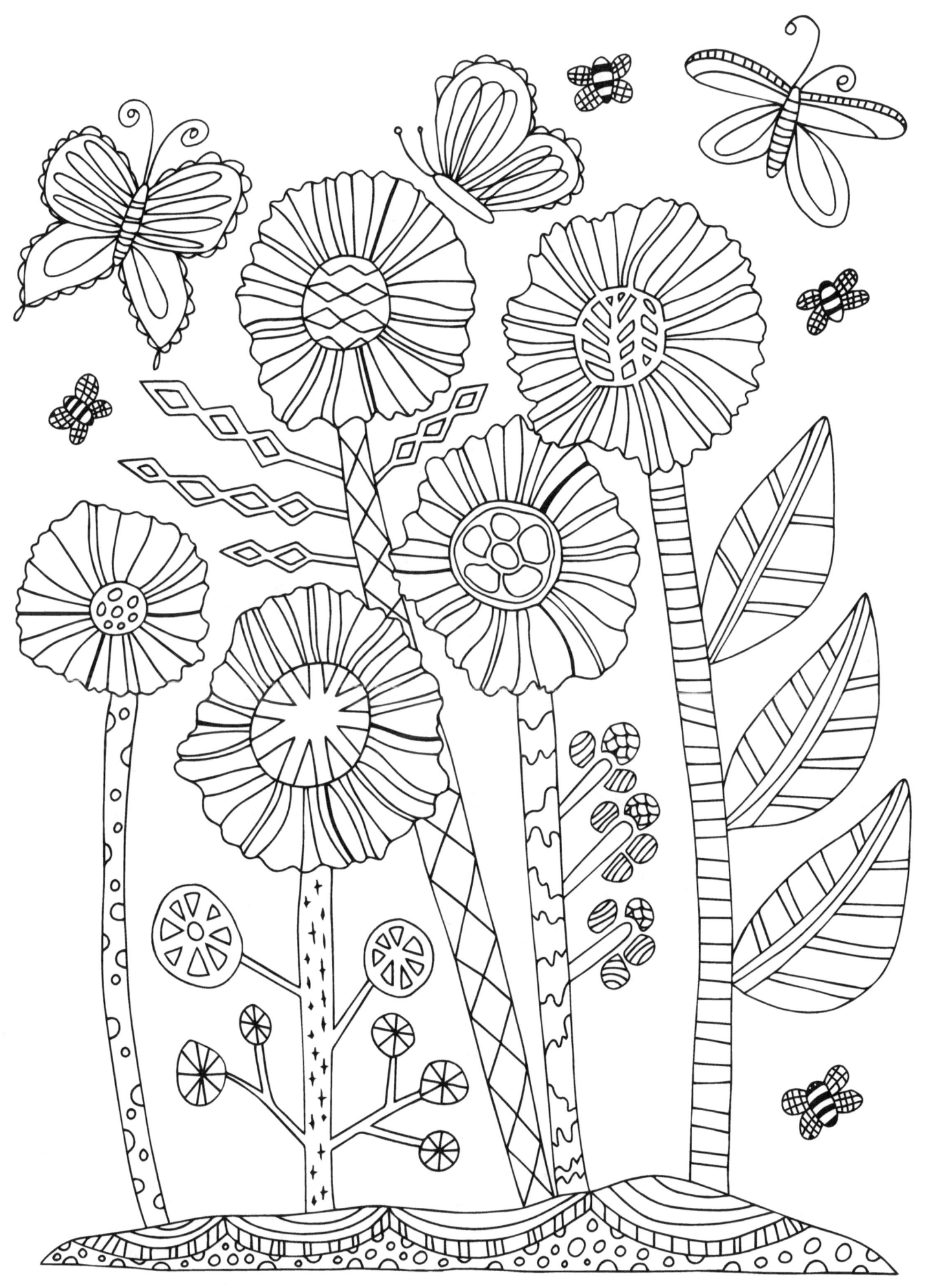

One way you would like to GROW in the next year?

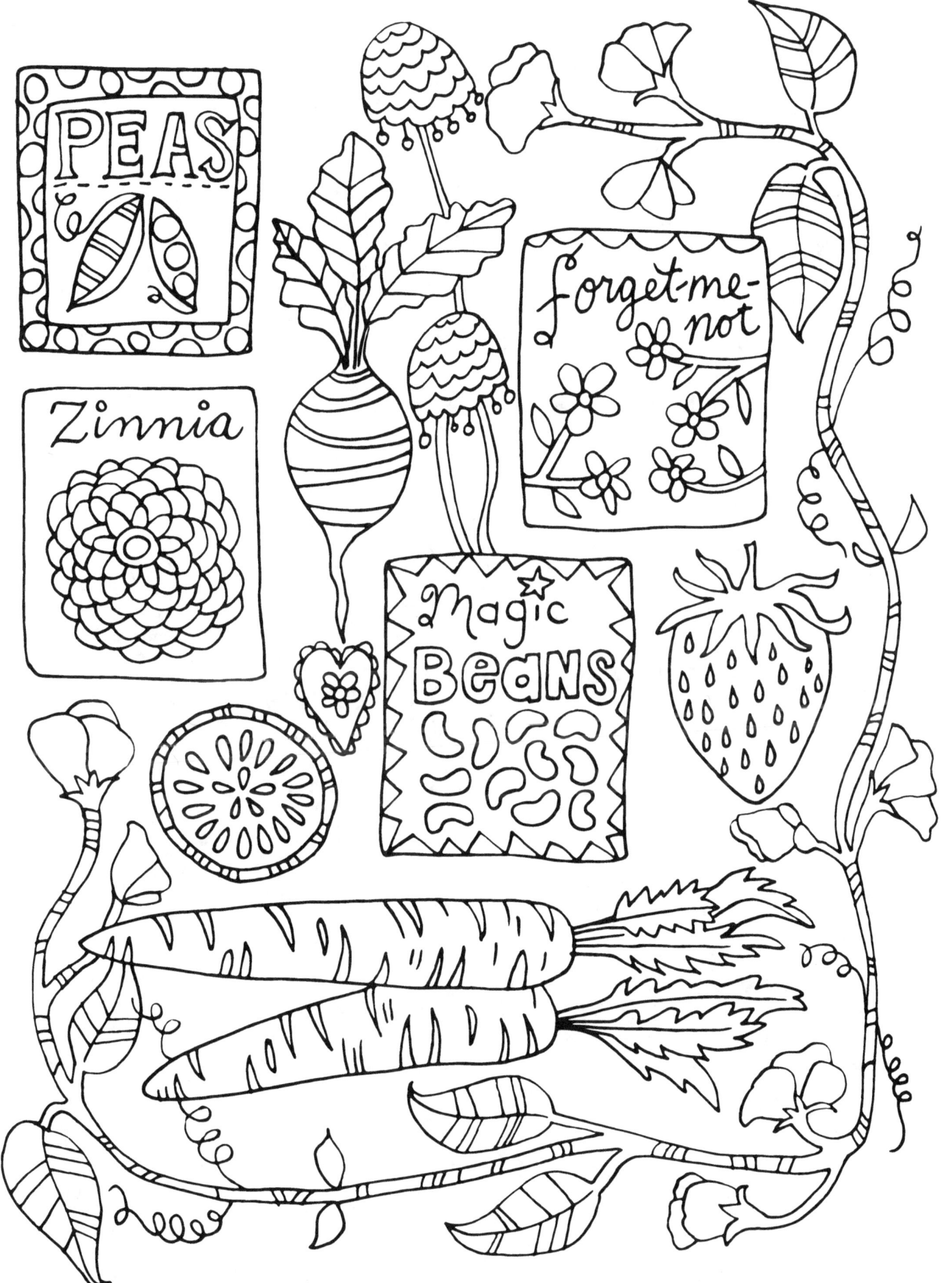

what's the best investment under [$100] you've made?

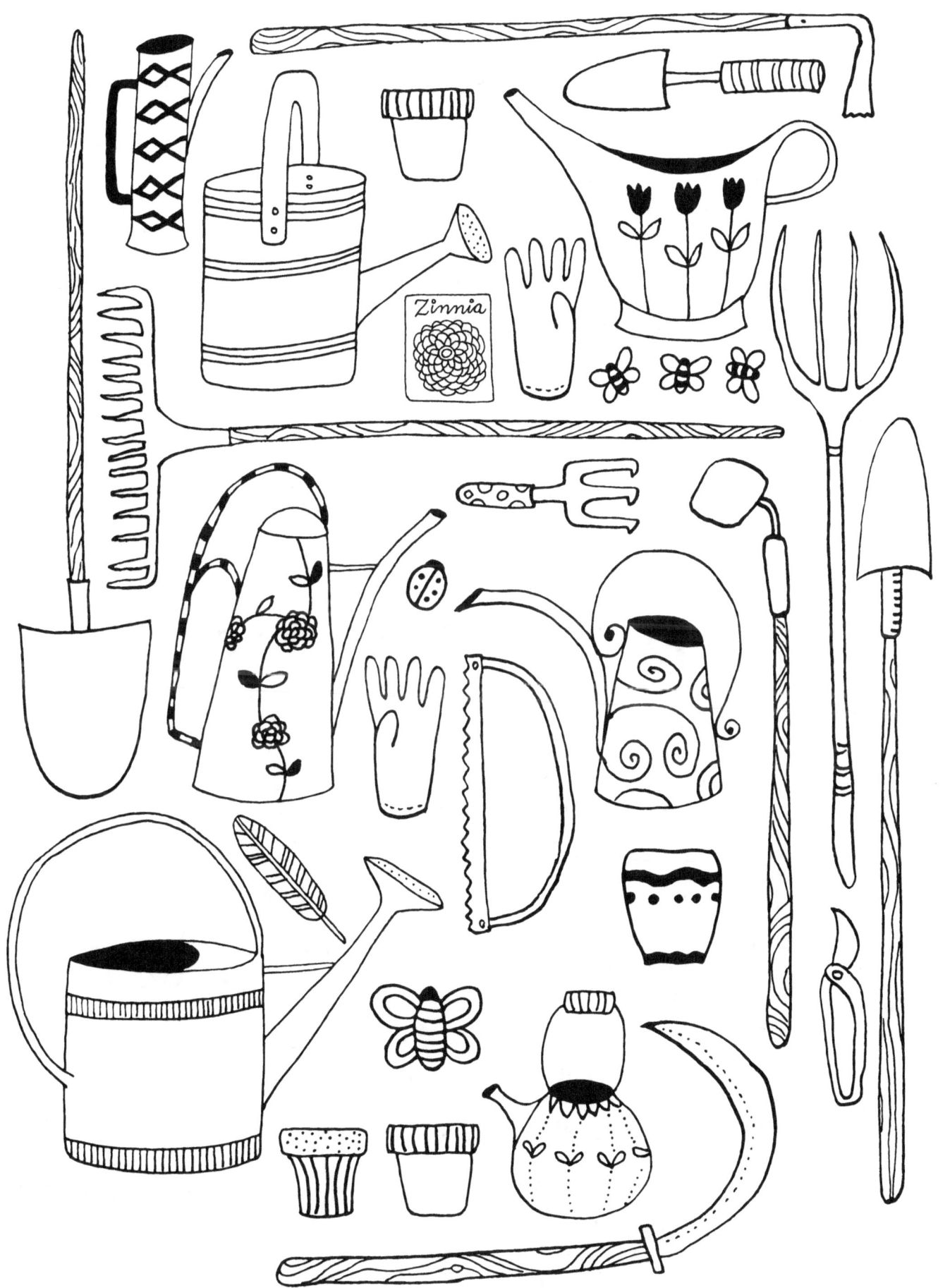

WHAT DID YOU LOVE TO DO AS A Child?

*this is key to what brings you happiness now.

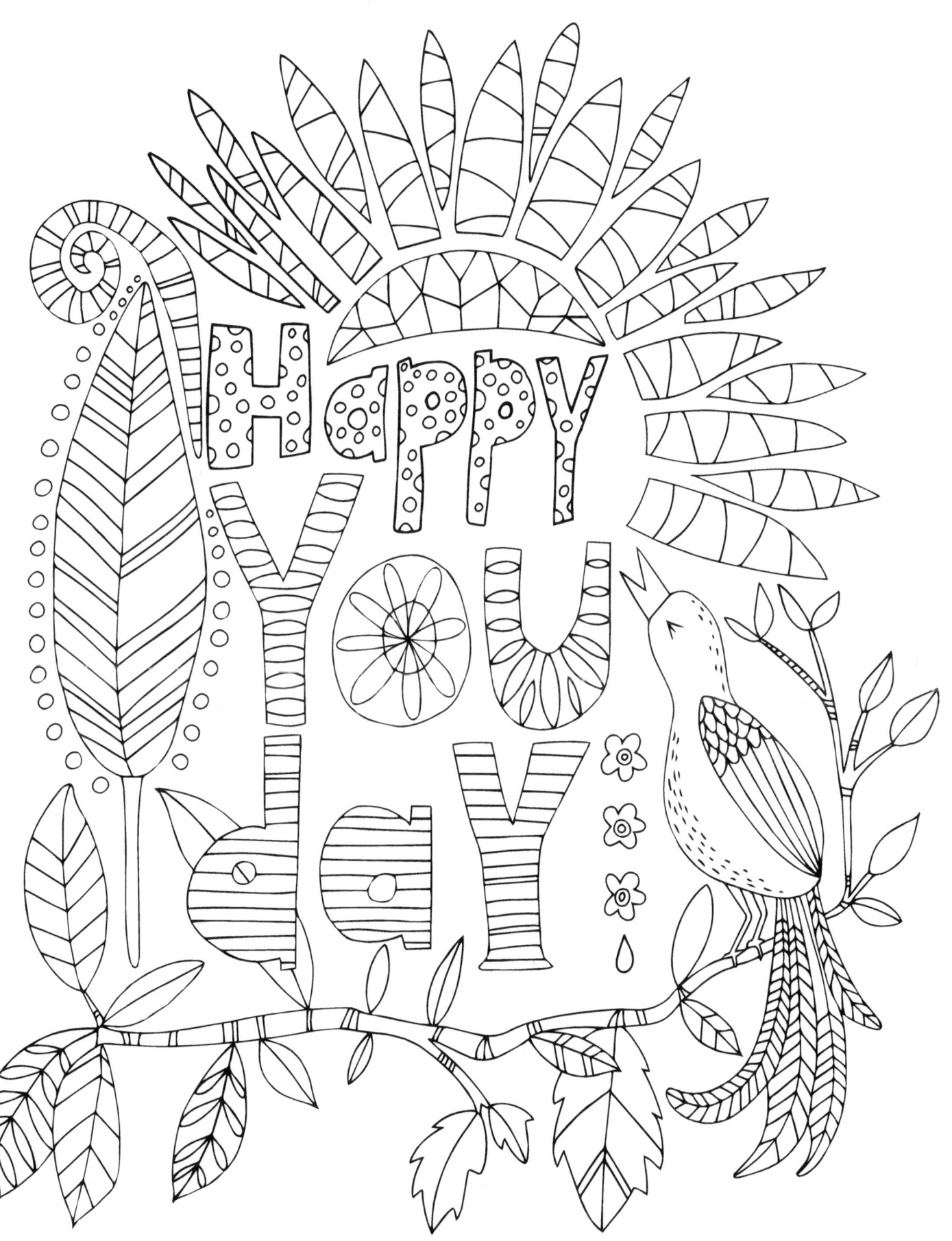

IF YOU COULD BE any ANIMAL what would you be? WHY?

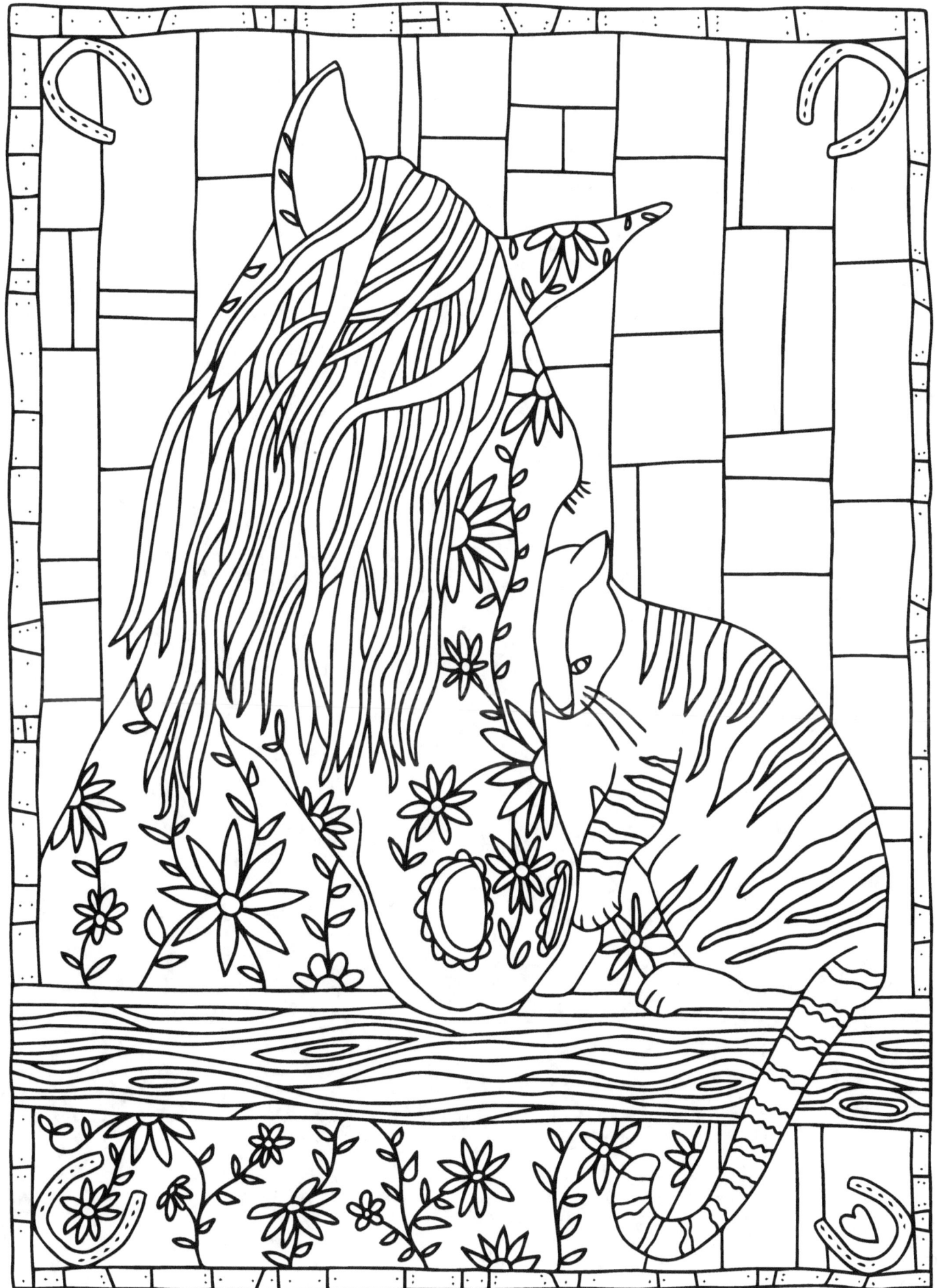

List 10 things that make you **HAPPY?**

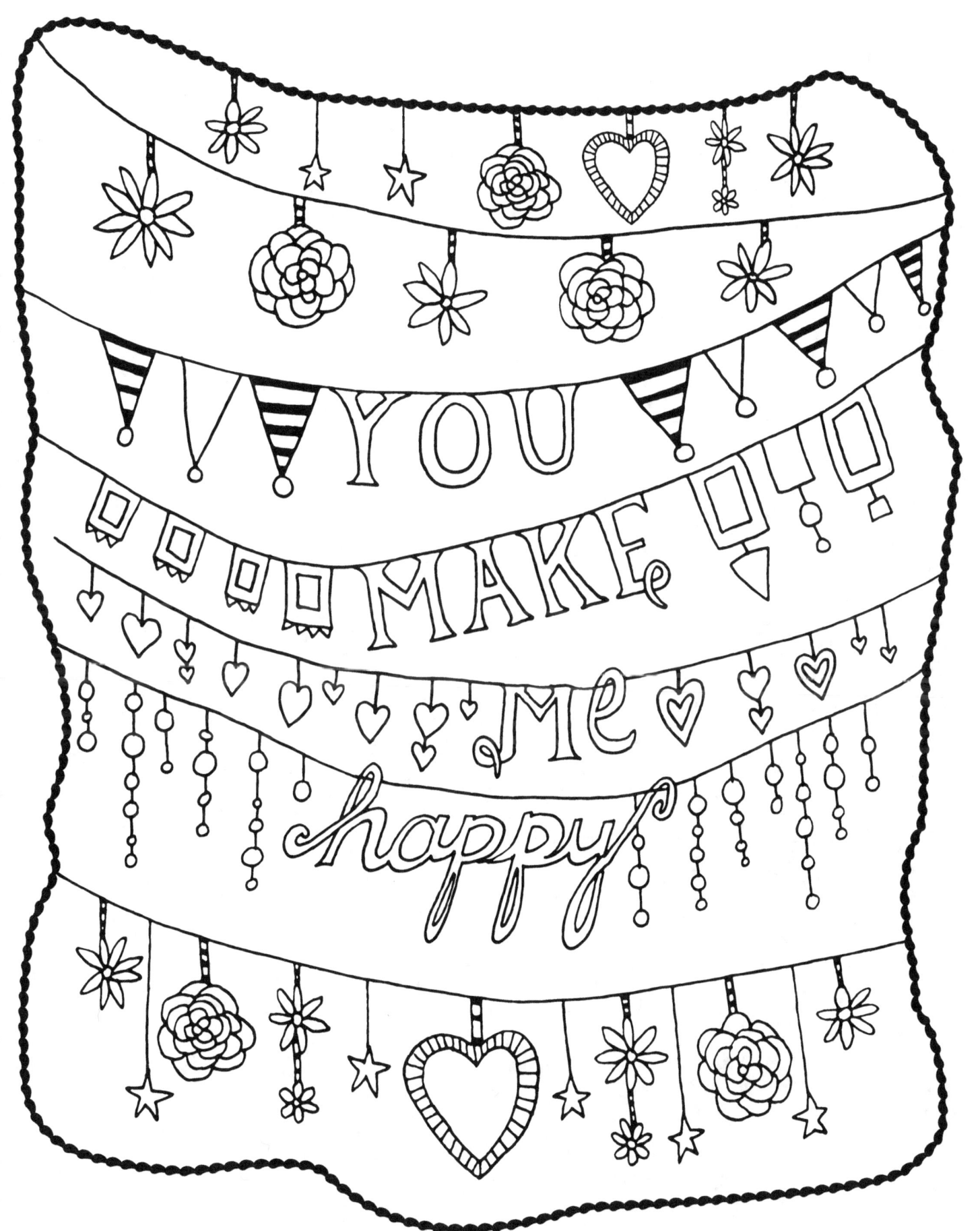

i
WANT TO
LEARN TO...

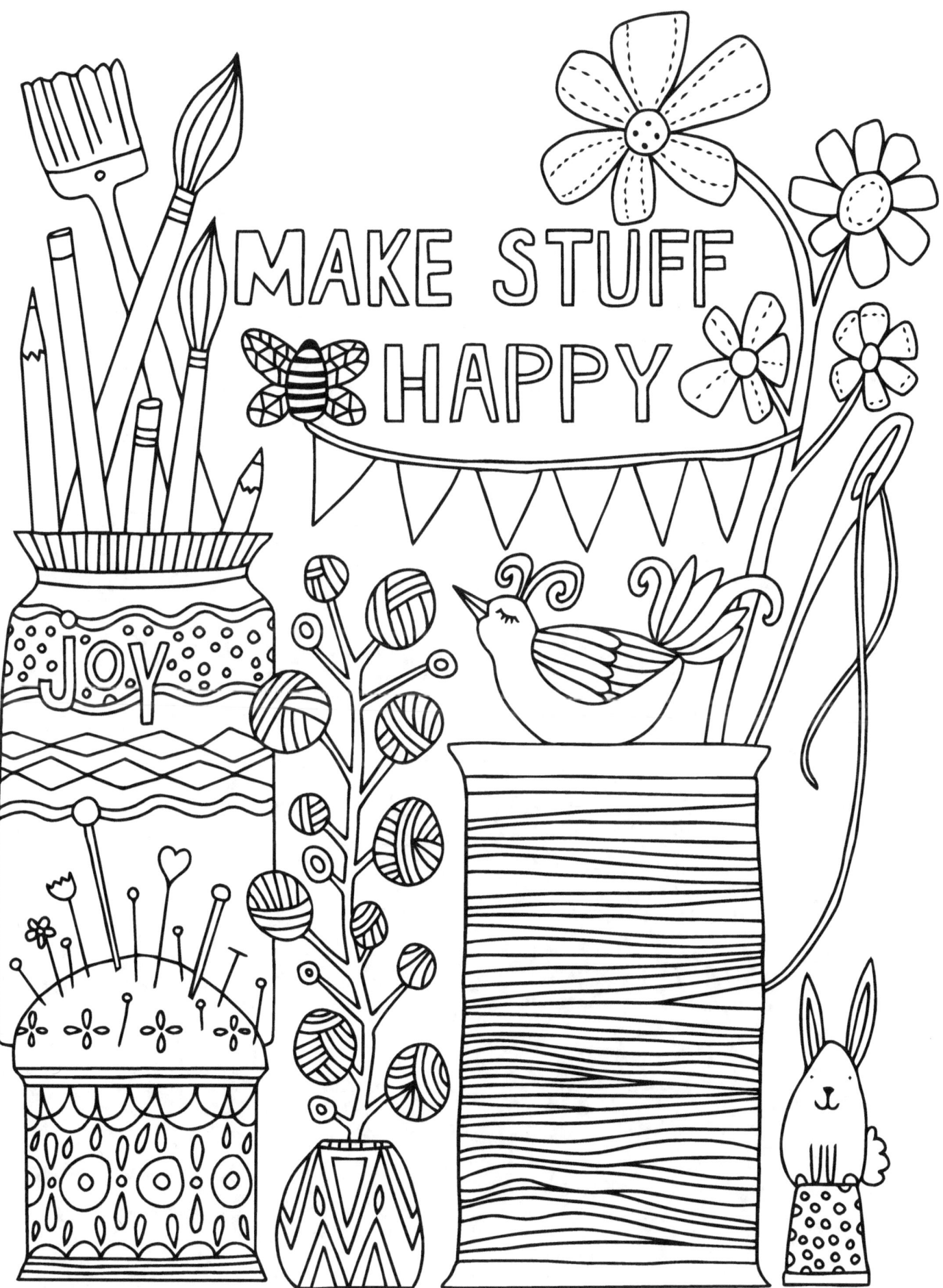

Dream vacation... where? when?

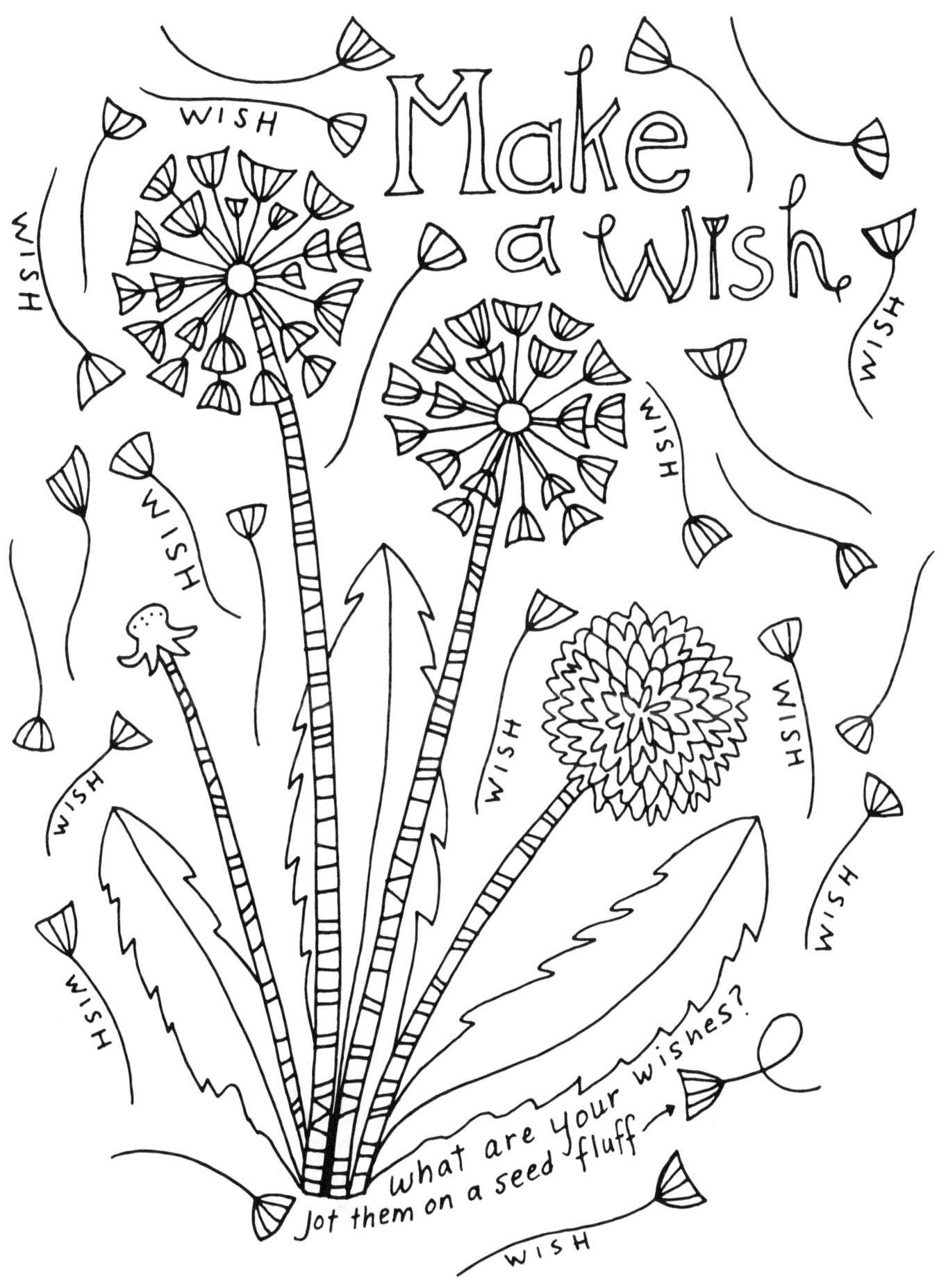

things I HAVE learned to love

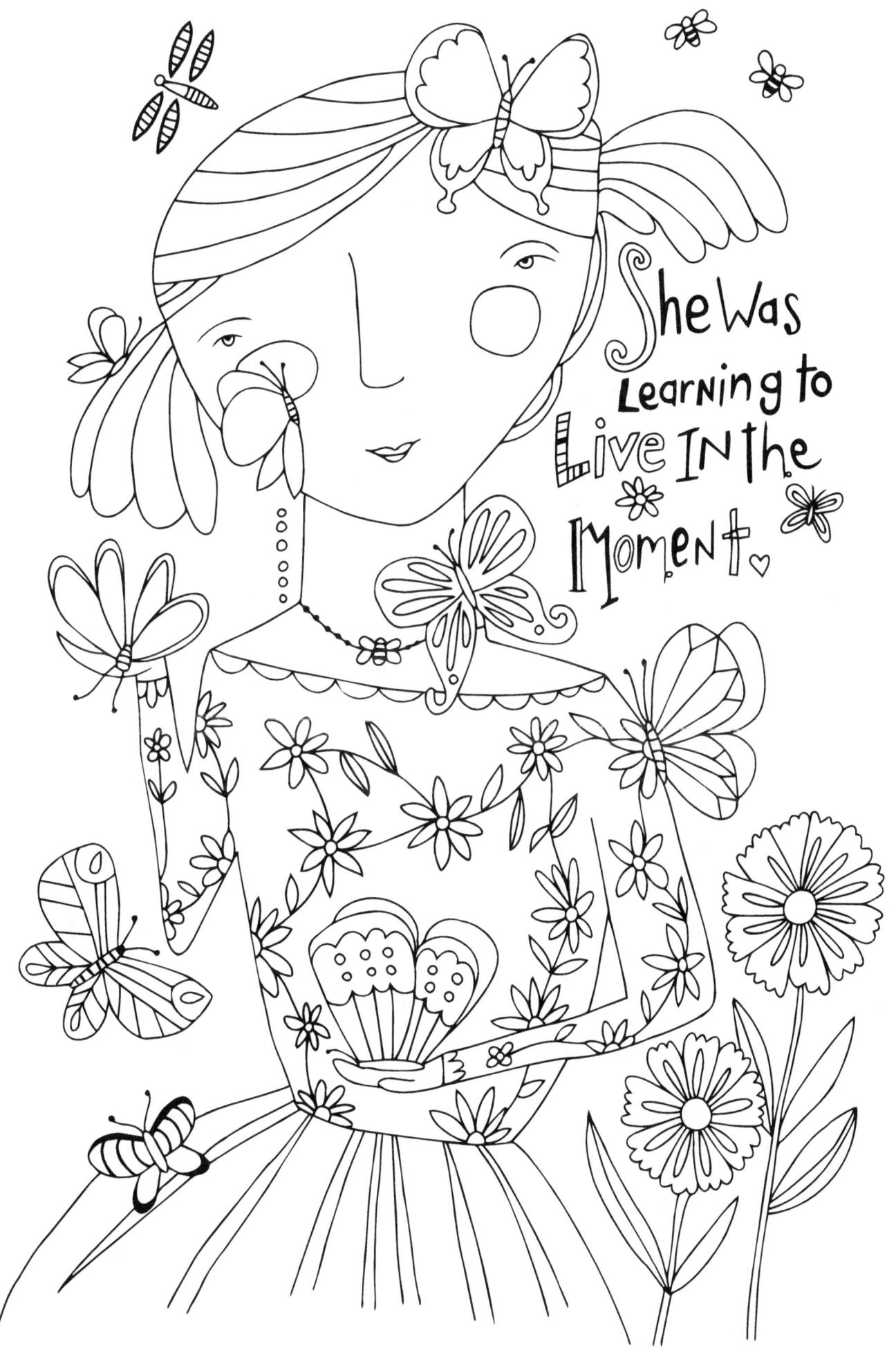

What are you ready to Let go?

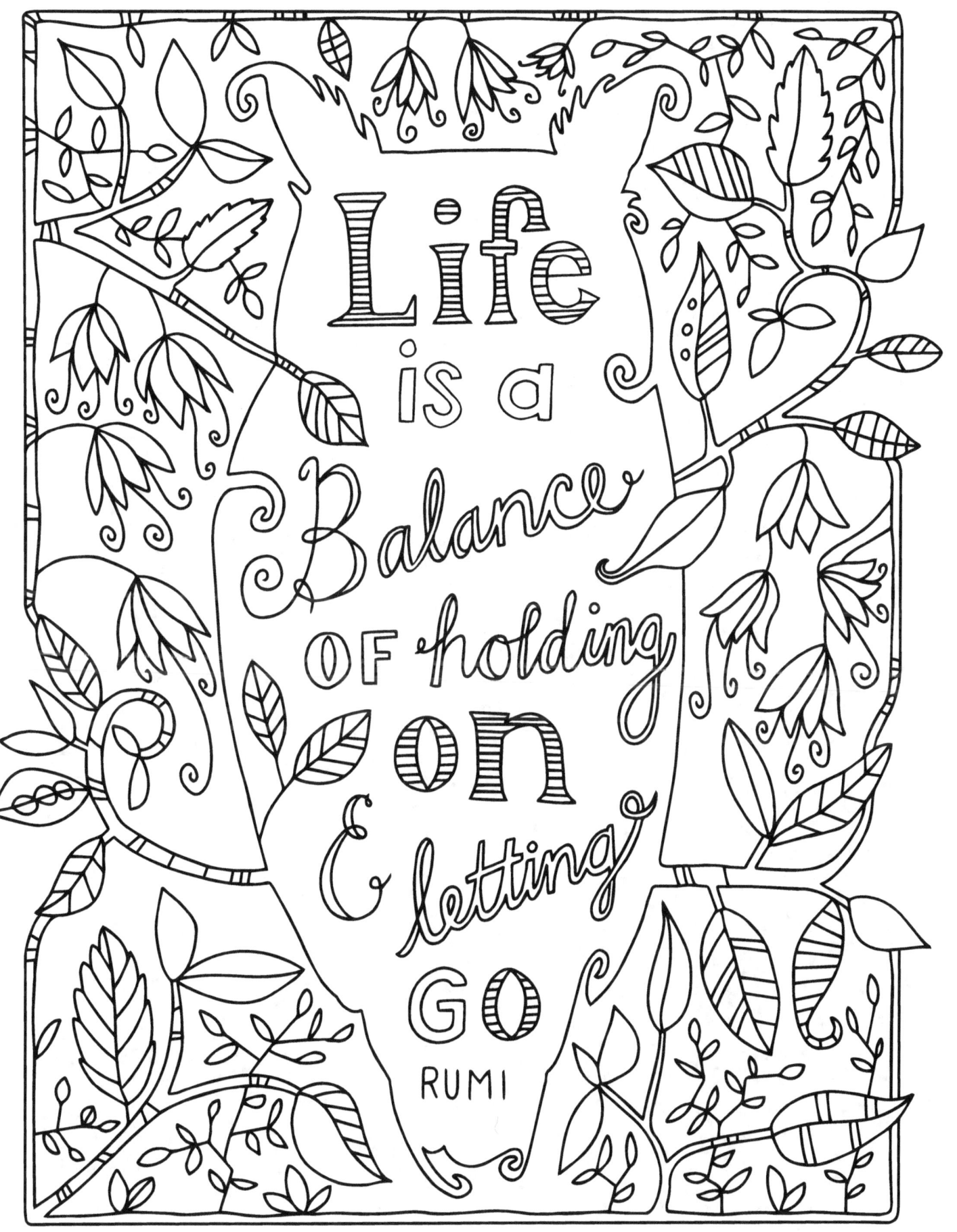

BOOKS
you love + would read again + again ♡

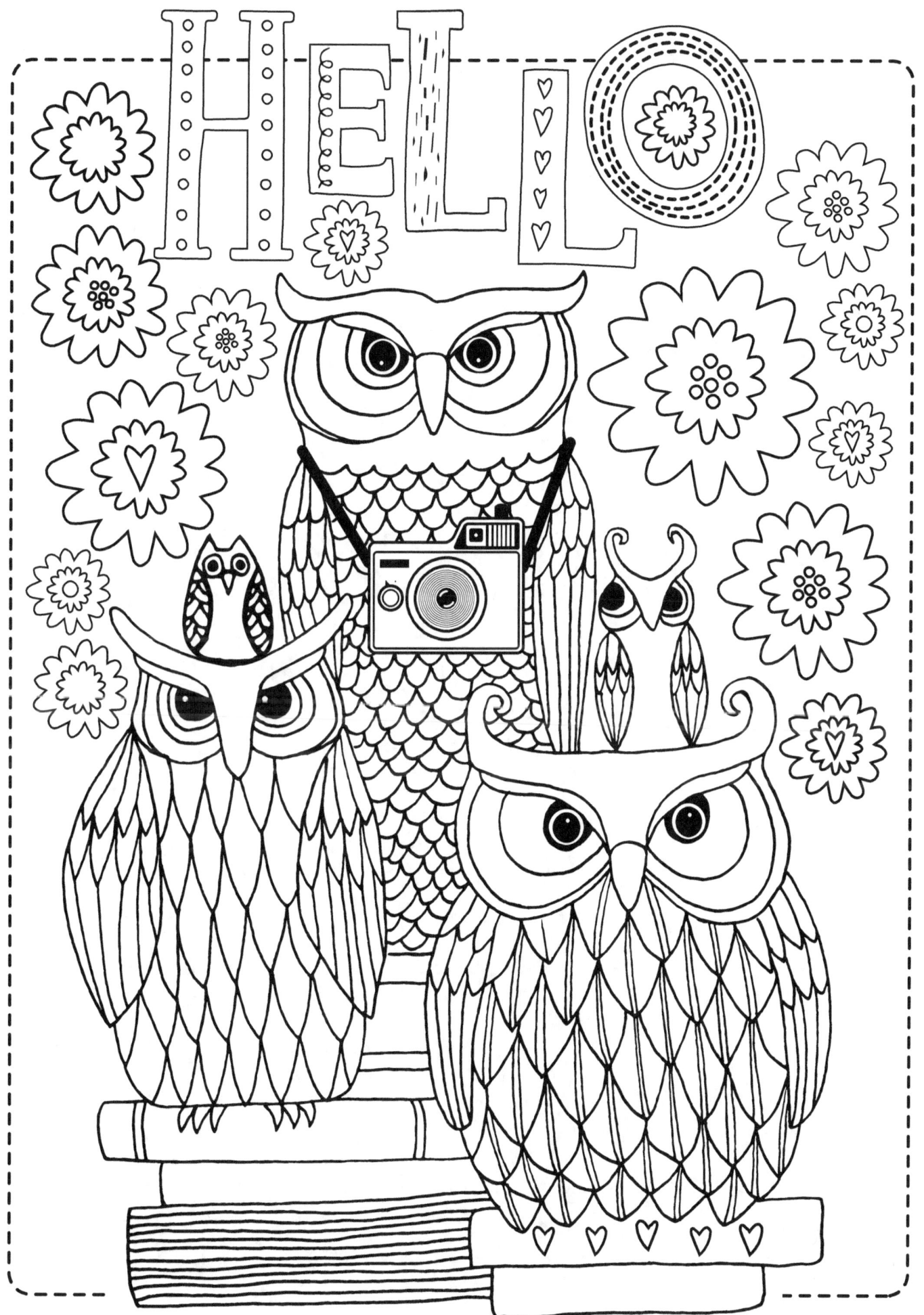

MY MOST FAVORITE WORDS
(or least favorite)

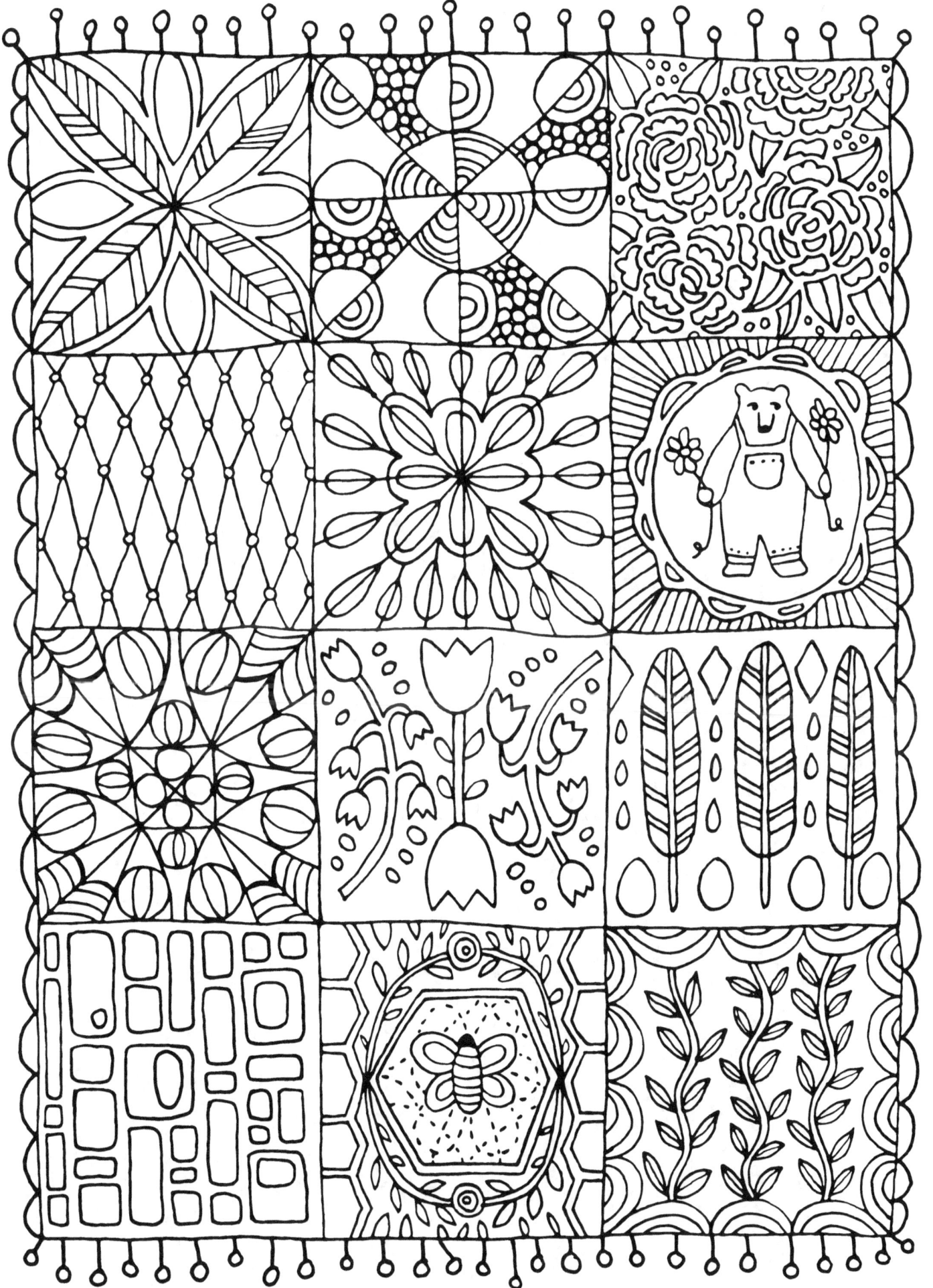

You are walking on a road and you encounter three paths.

⛰ One path leads up a mountain.

🌲 The other leads into a forest.

〰 The third path leads to the ocean.

Which path would you choose... why?

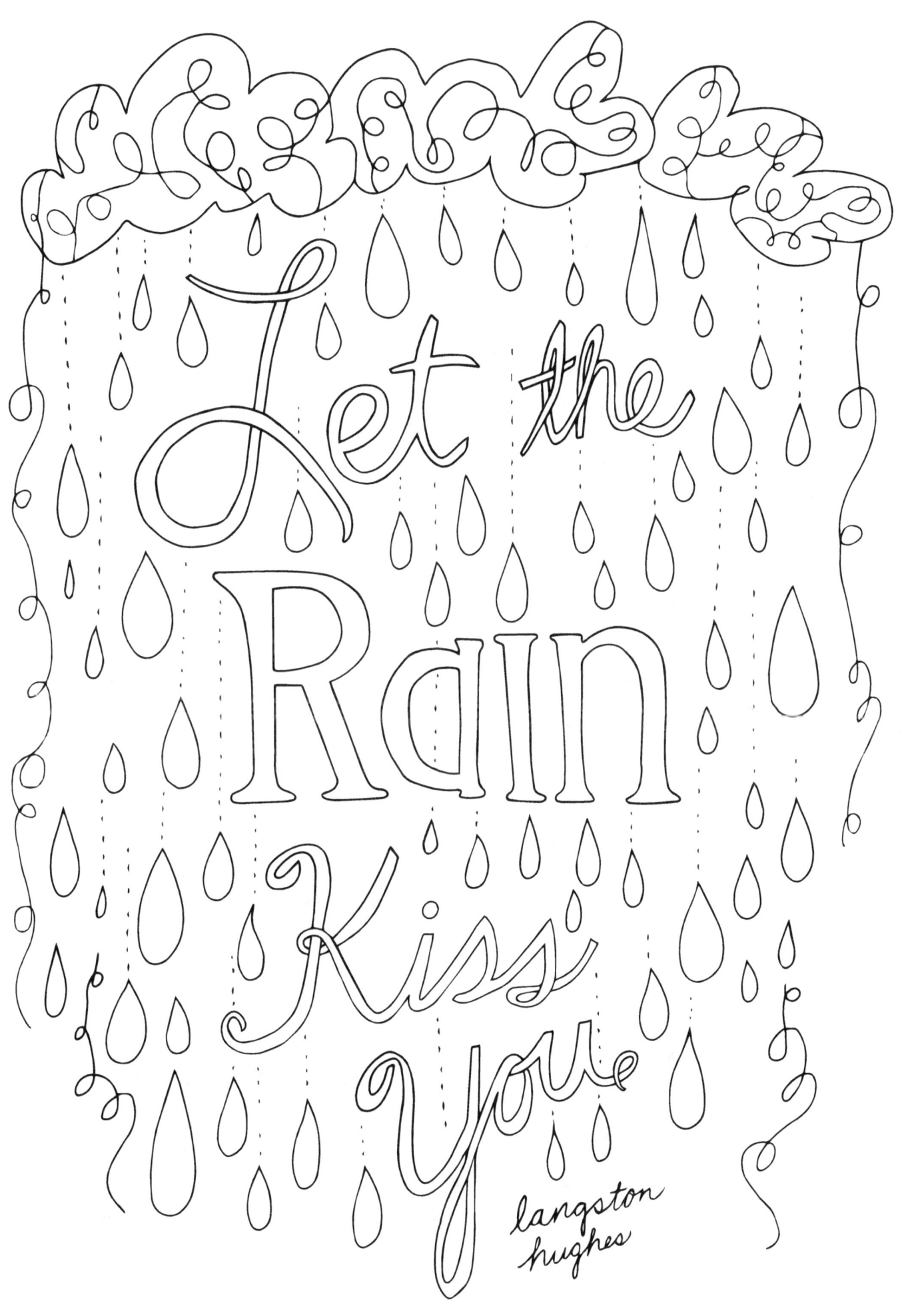

What do you DO to CHEER yourself UP?

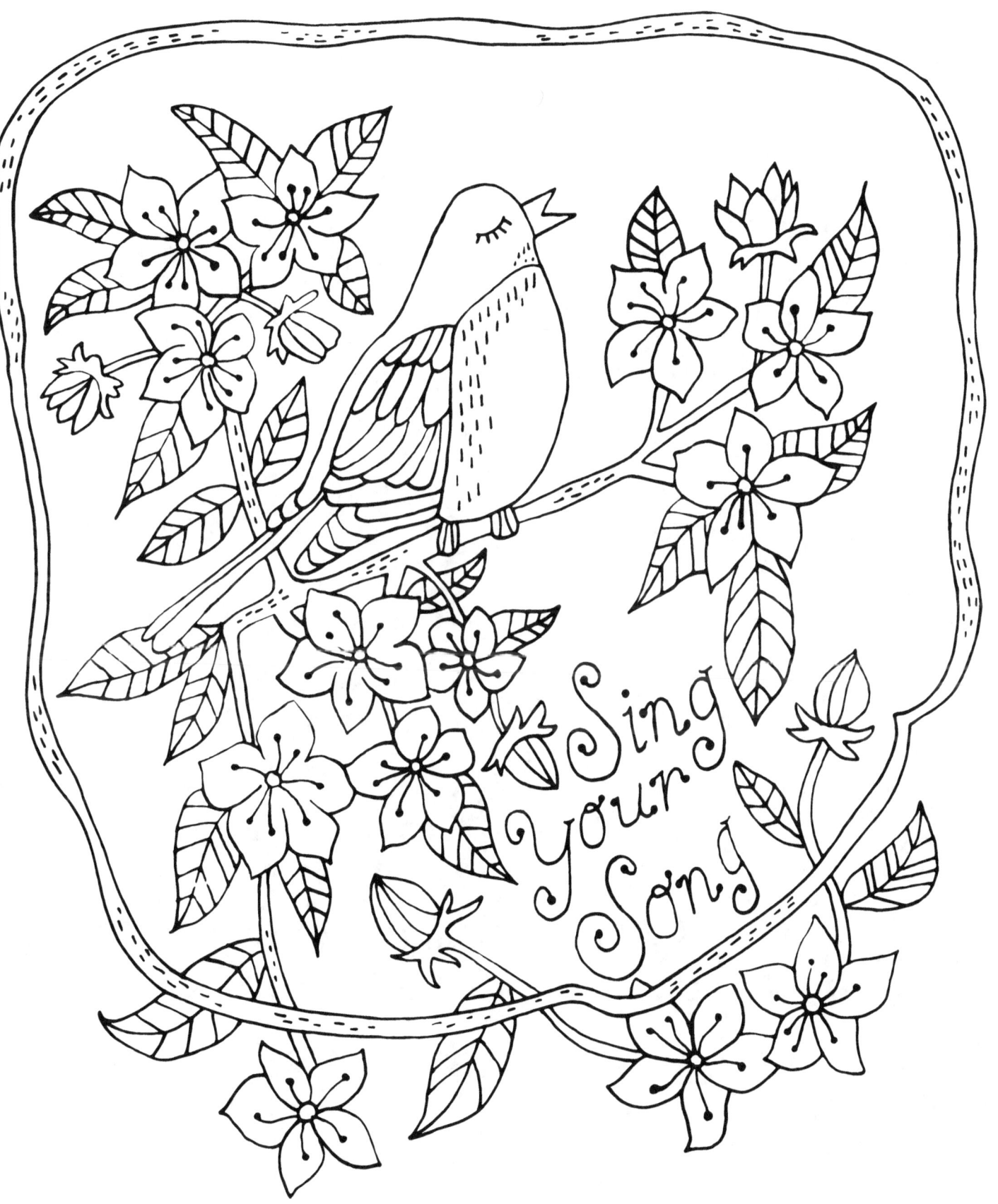

What's your Dream H♥ME?

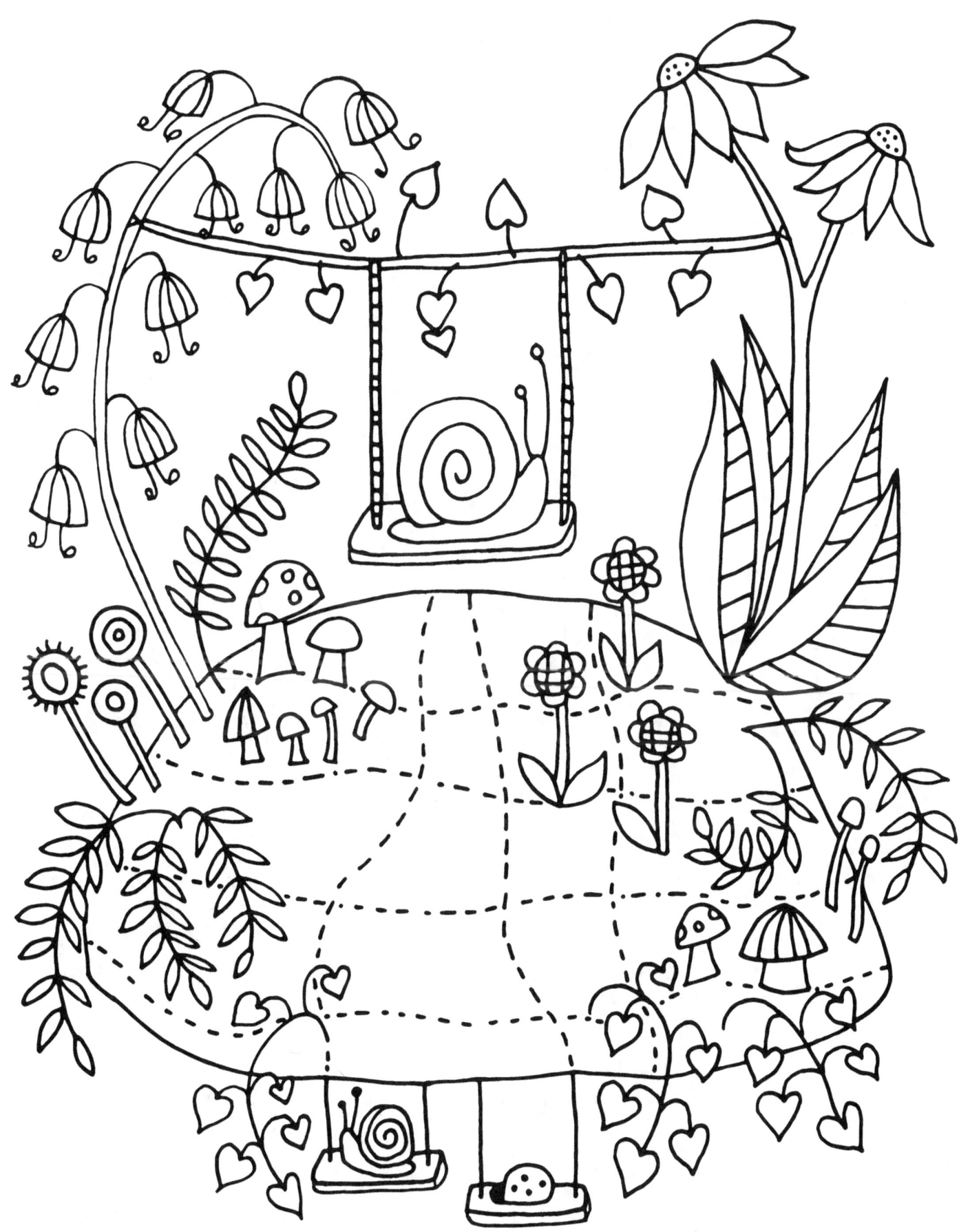

If you could
go back in time
and change
One thing
from your Past...

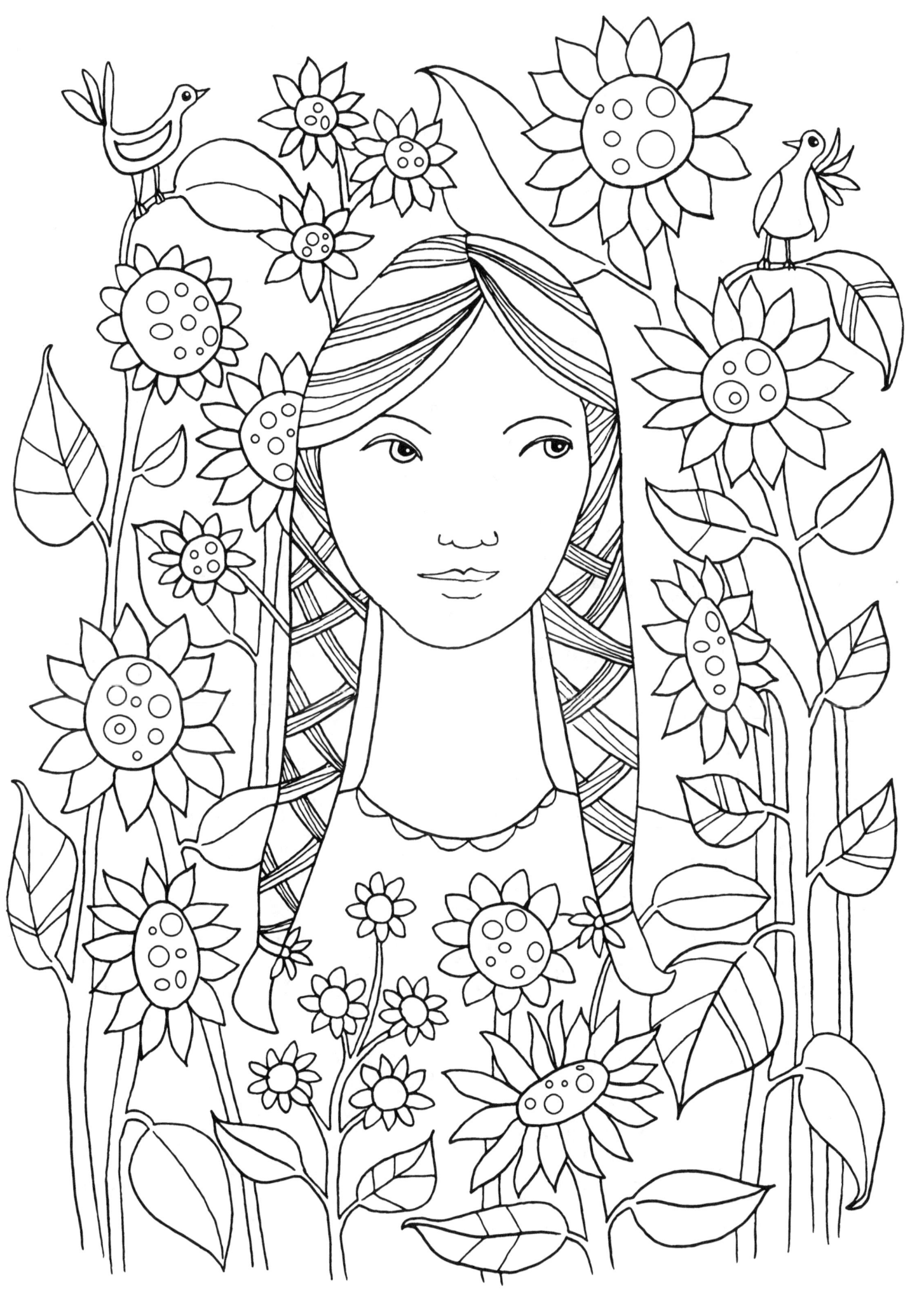

the
most
FUN
i
have
ever
had...

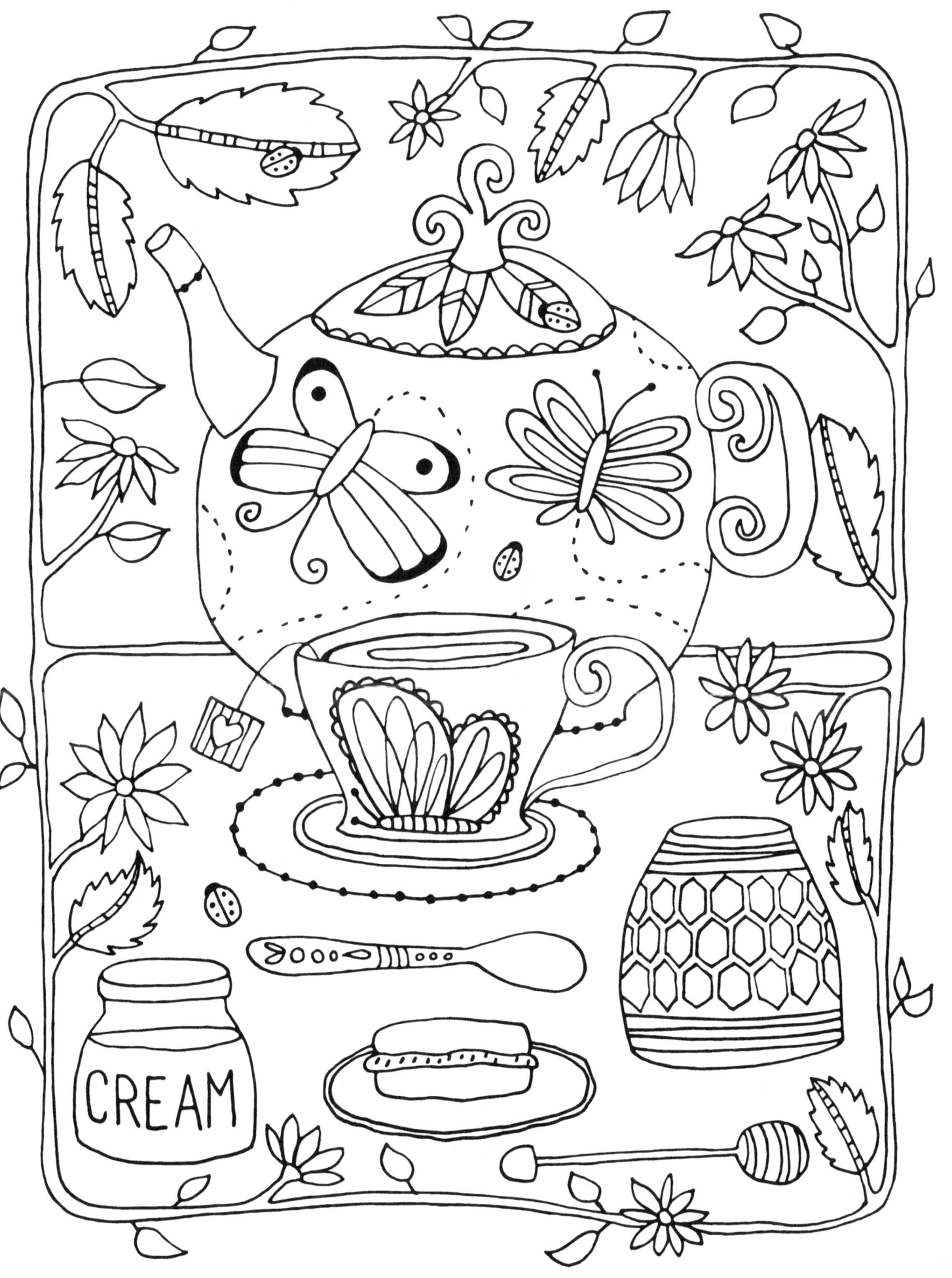

City Mouse or a County Mouse?

WHICH ARE YOU?

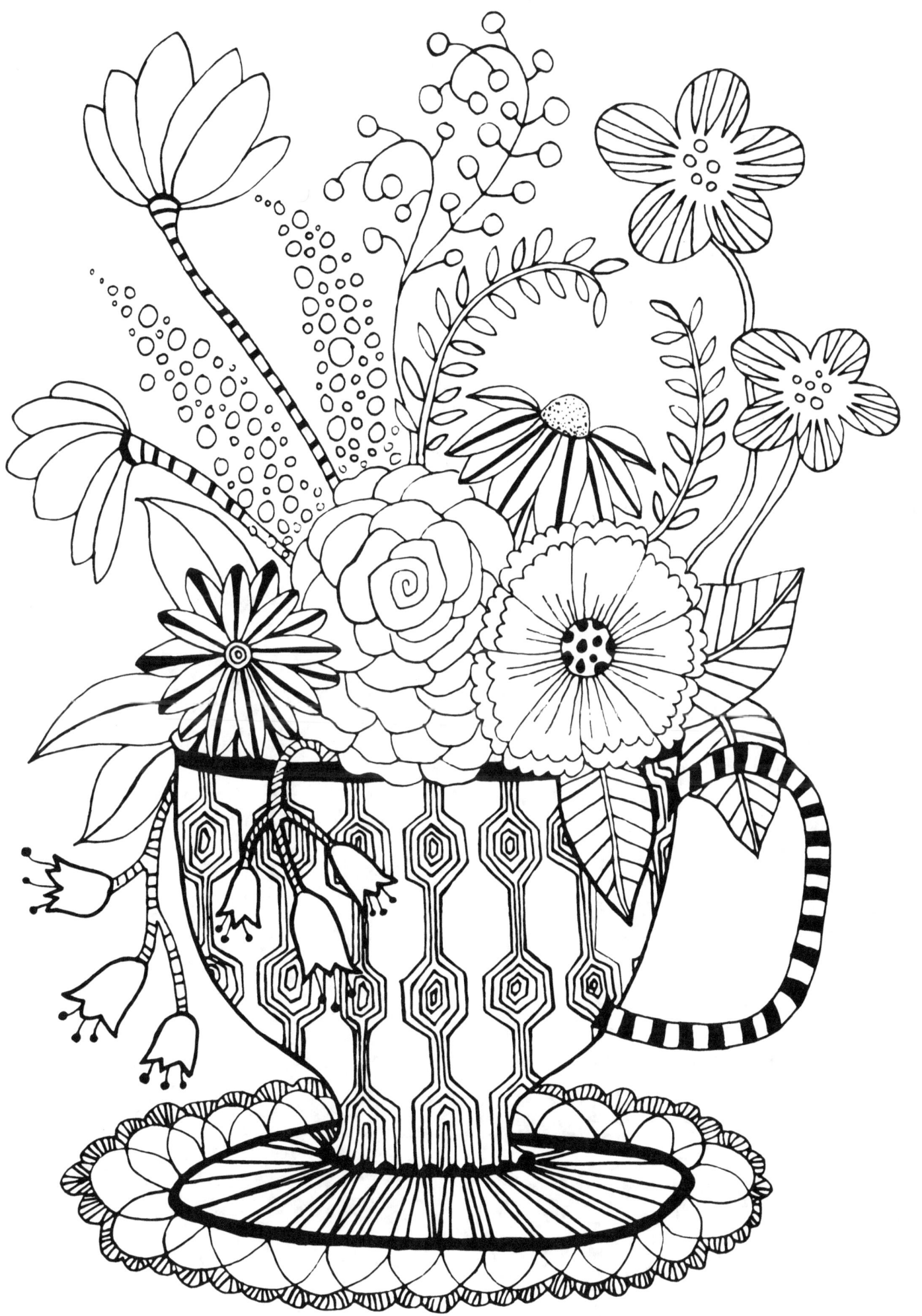

3
pet peeves

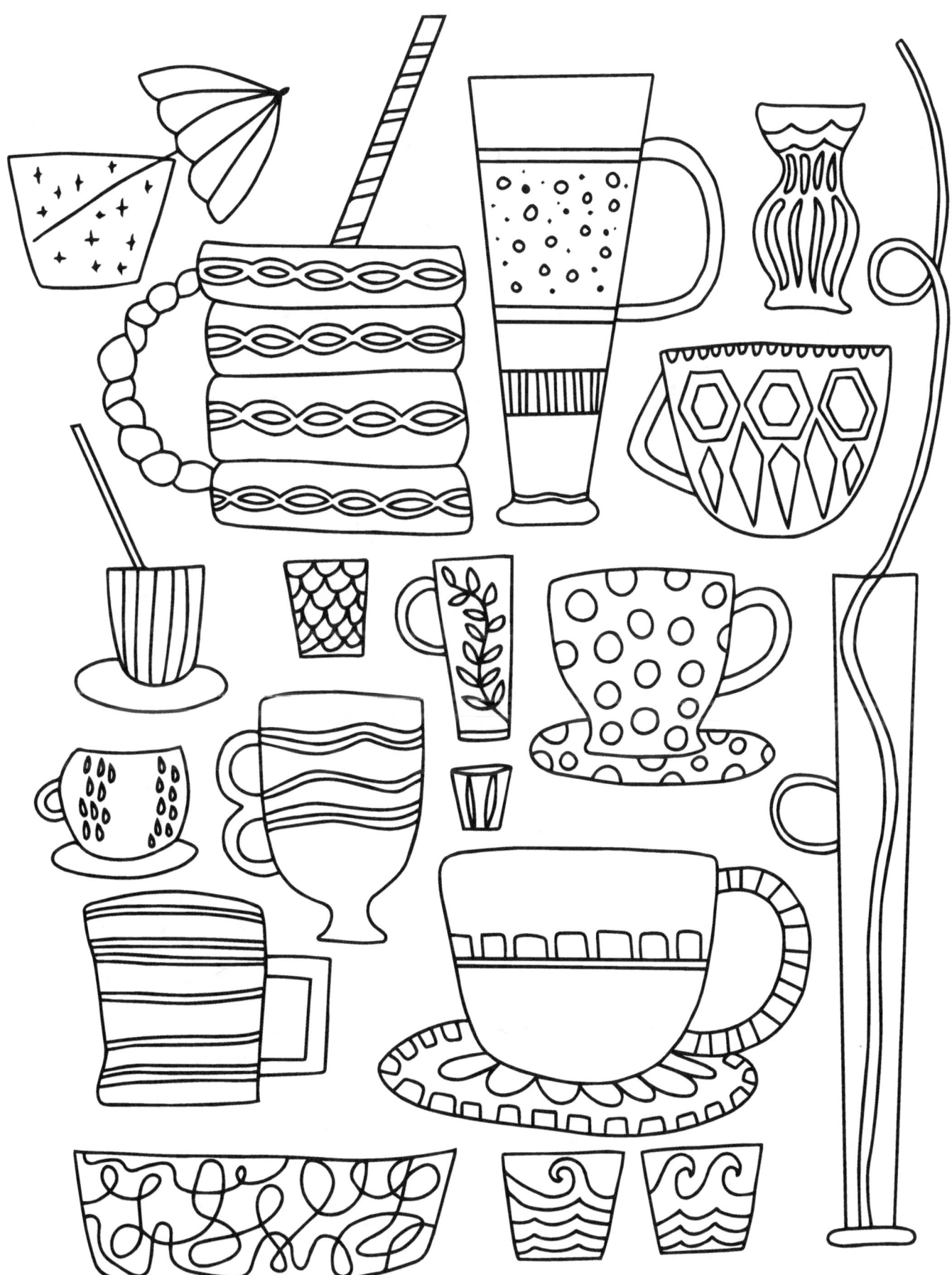

What do you **Wish** YOU HAD MORE **Time** FOR...

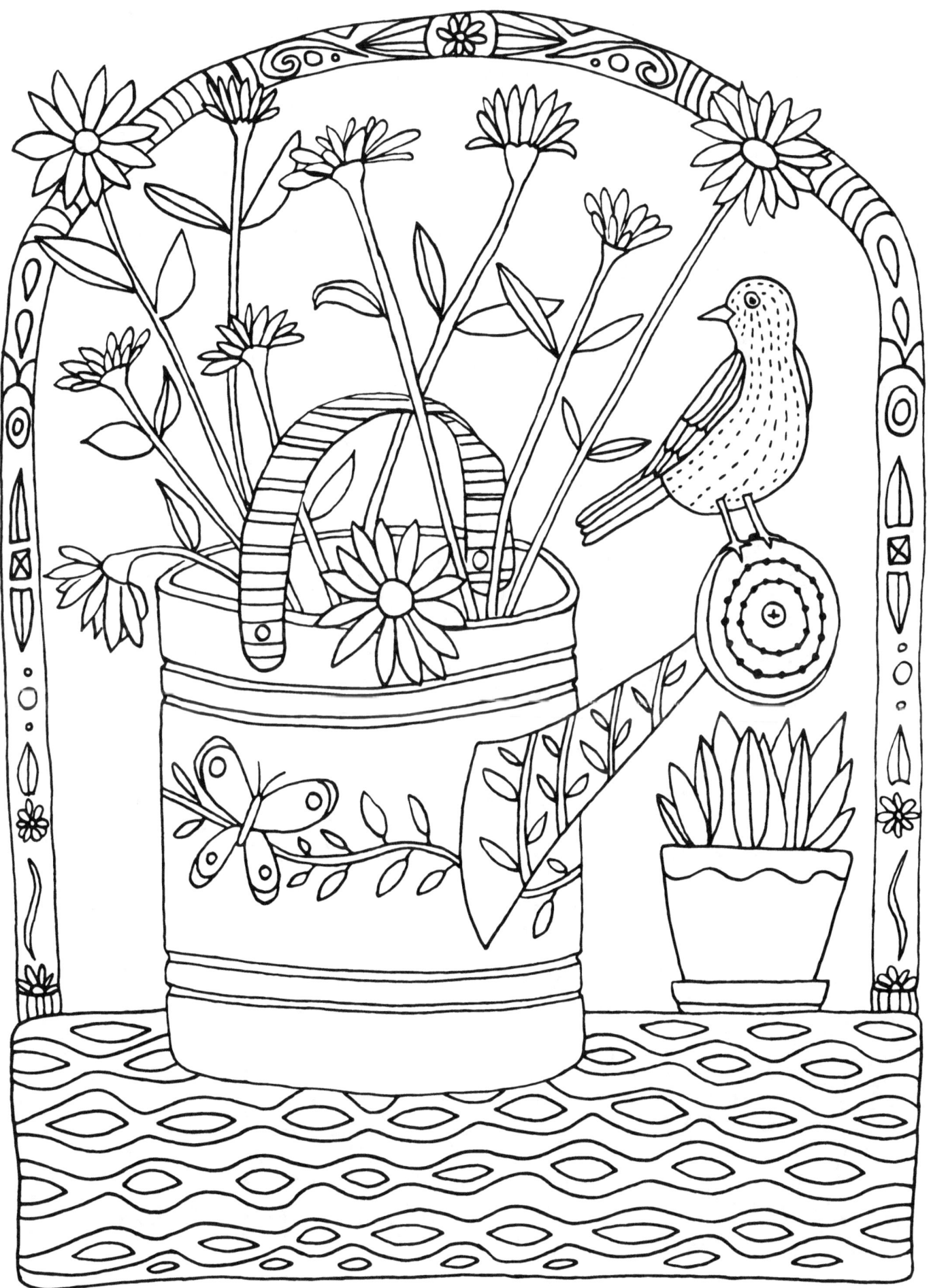

Never Stop exploring

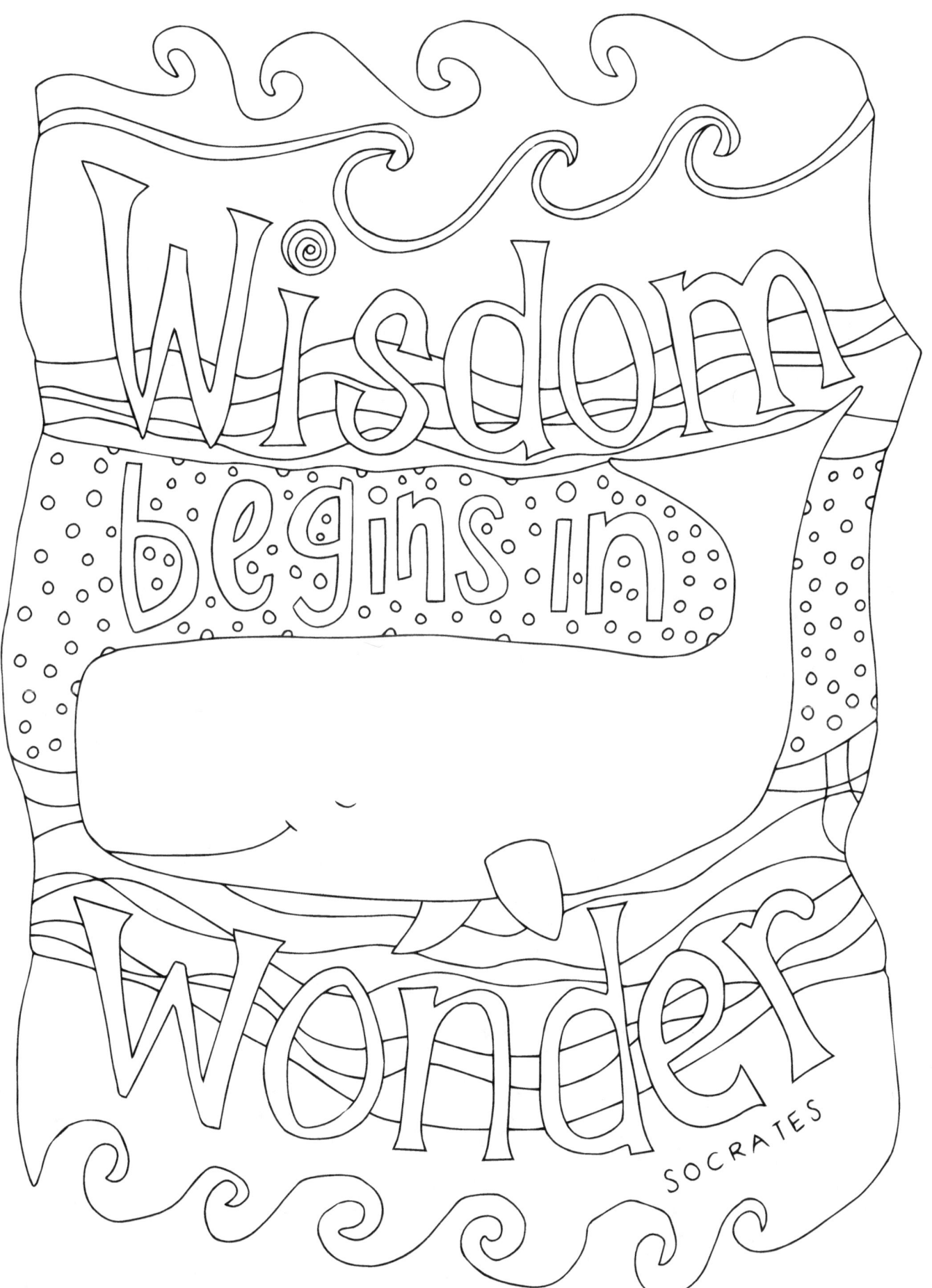

things I learned from my Mom or Dad...

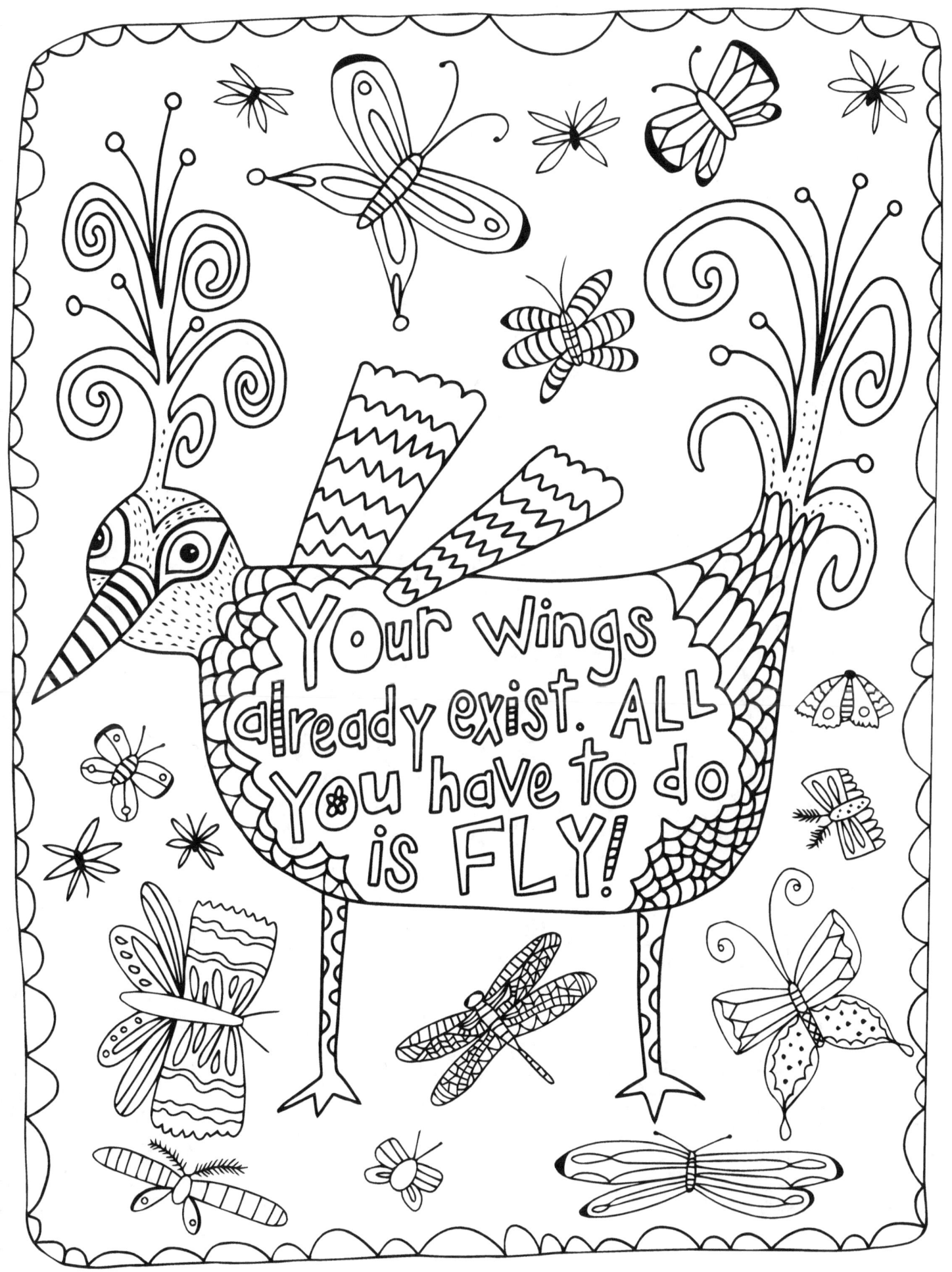

Someone that you ♥ MISS

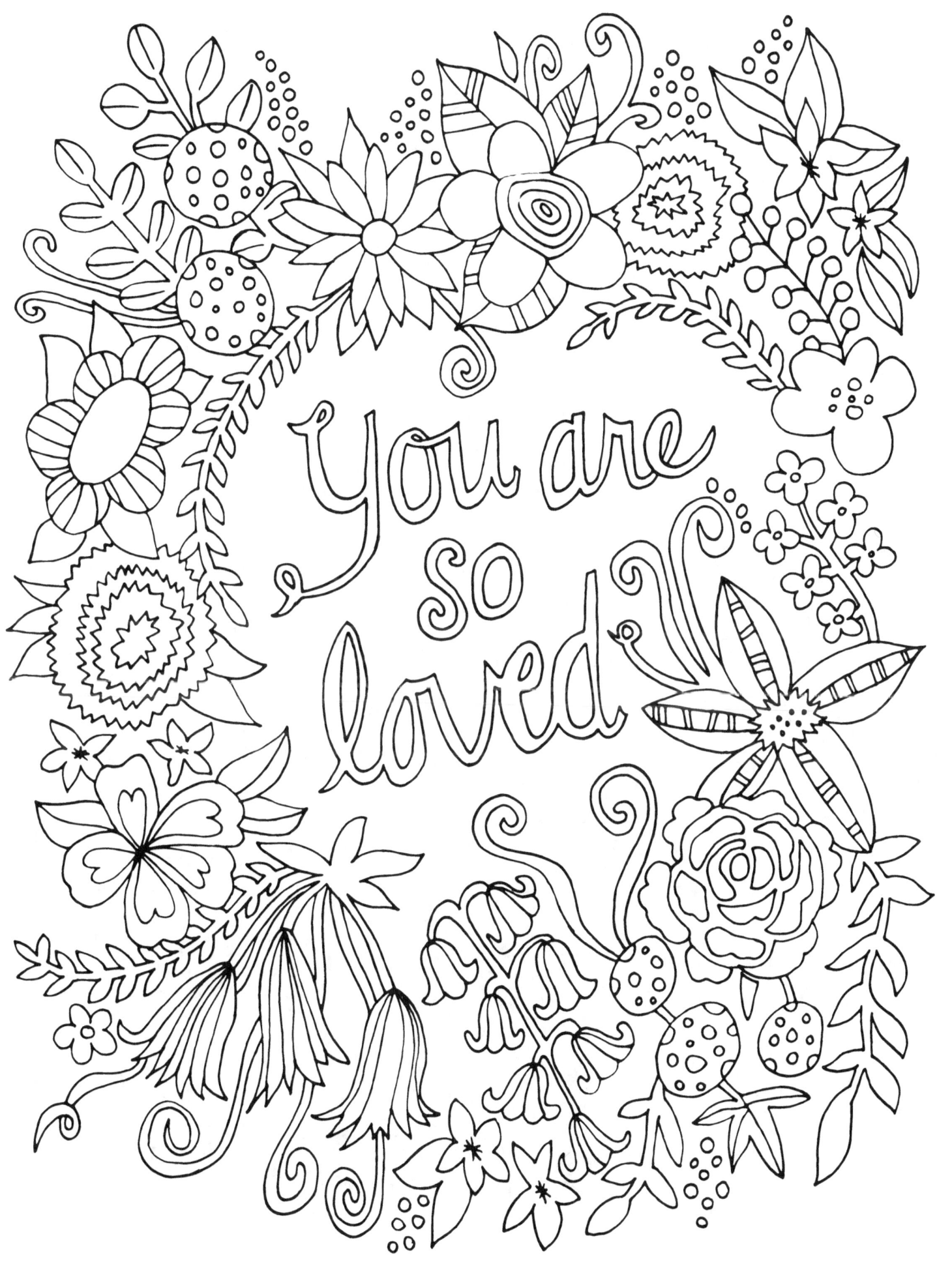

Color the backside of this page. Jot a quick note and send to a friend.
(it will make their day :))

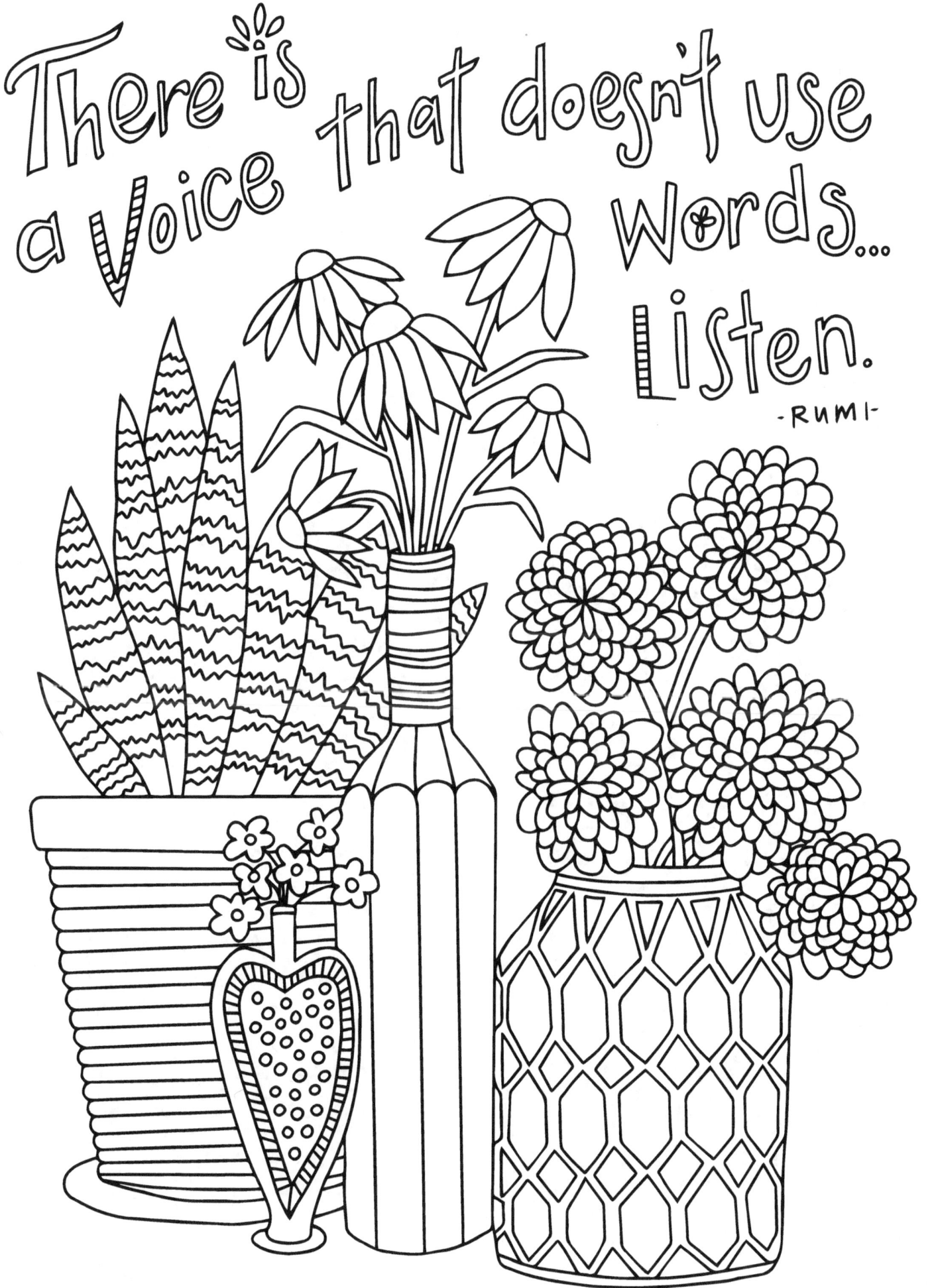

If you could change 1 thing about yourself, what would it be?

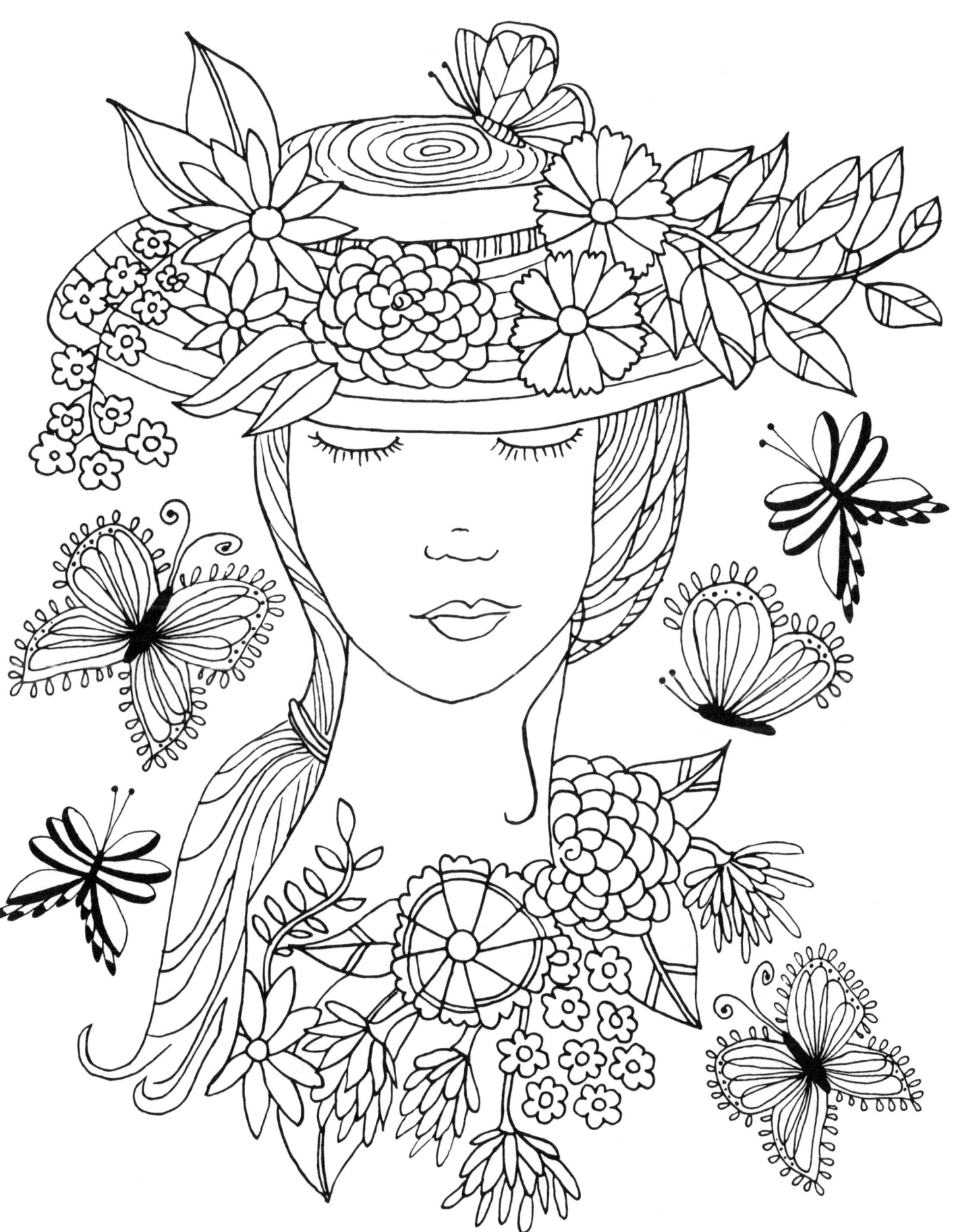

WHAT SCARES YOU?

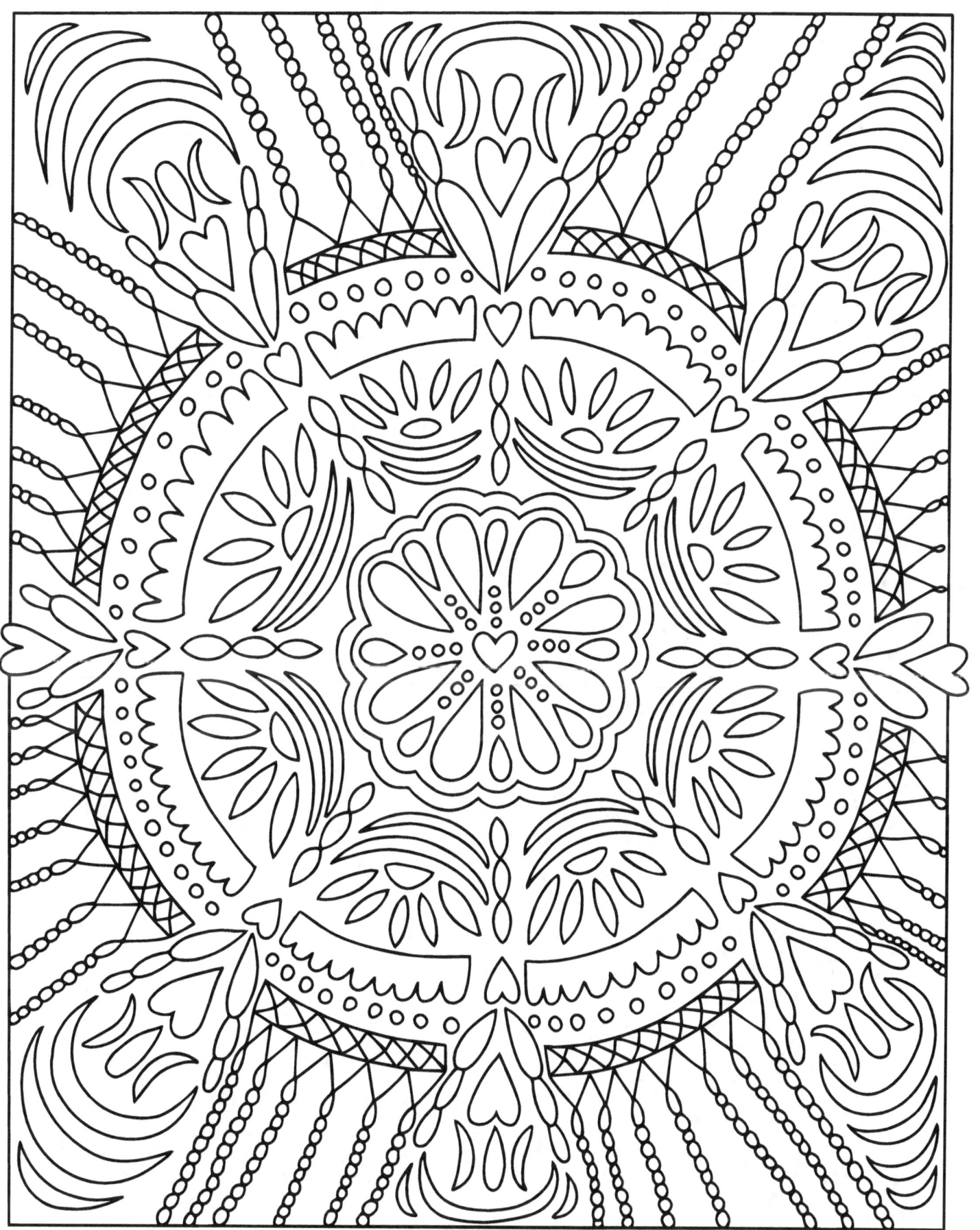

WHAT
*DO YOU
WANT TO DO
WHEN YOU
RETIRE?

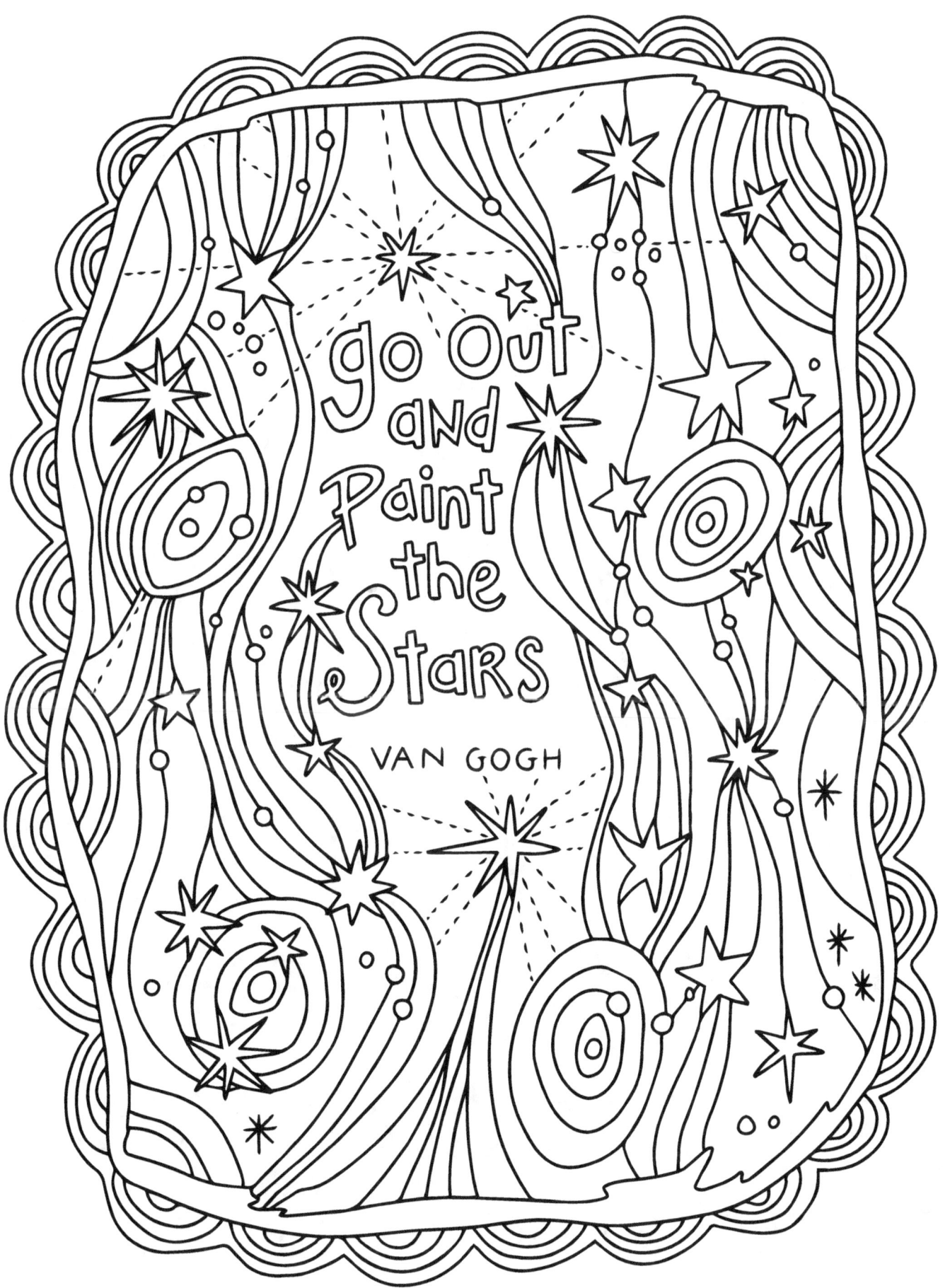

5 WEIRD THINGS *you like*

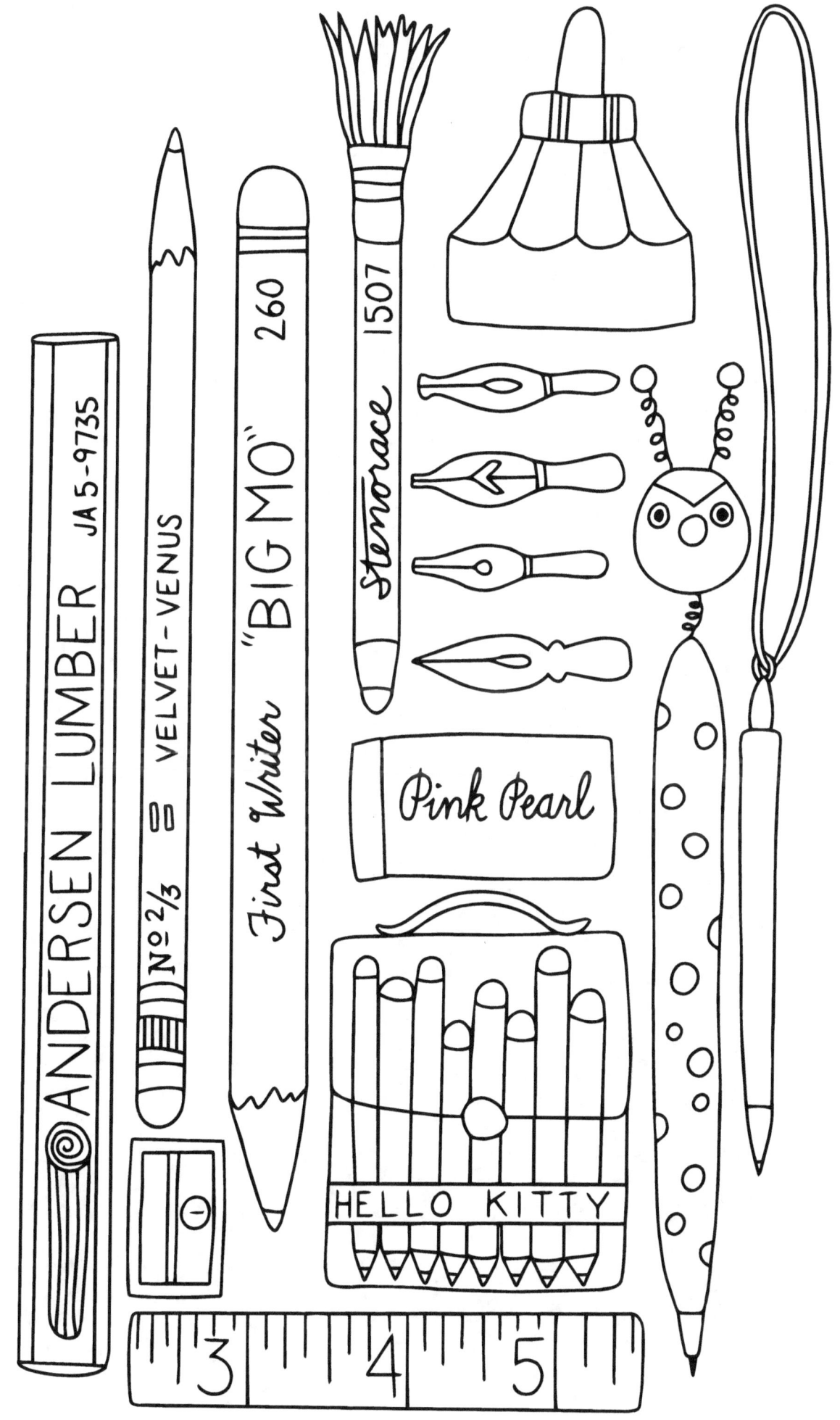

How would you Describe Yourself?

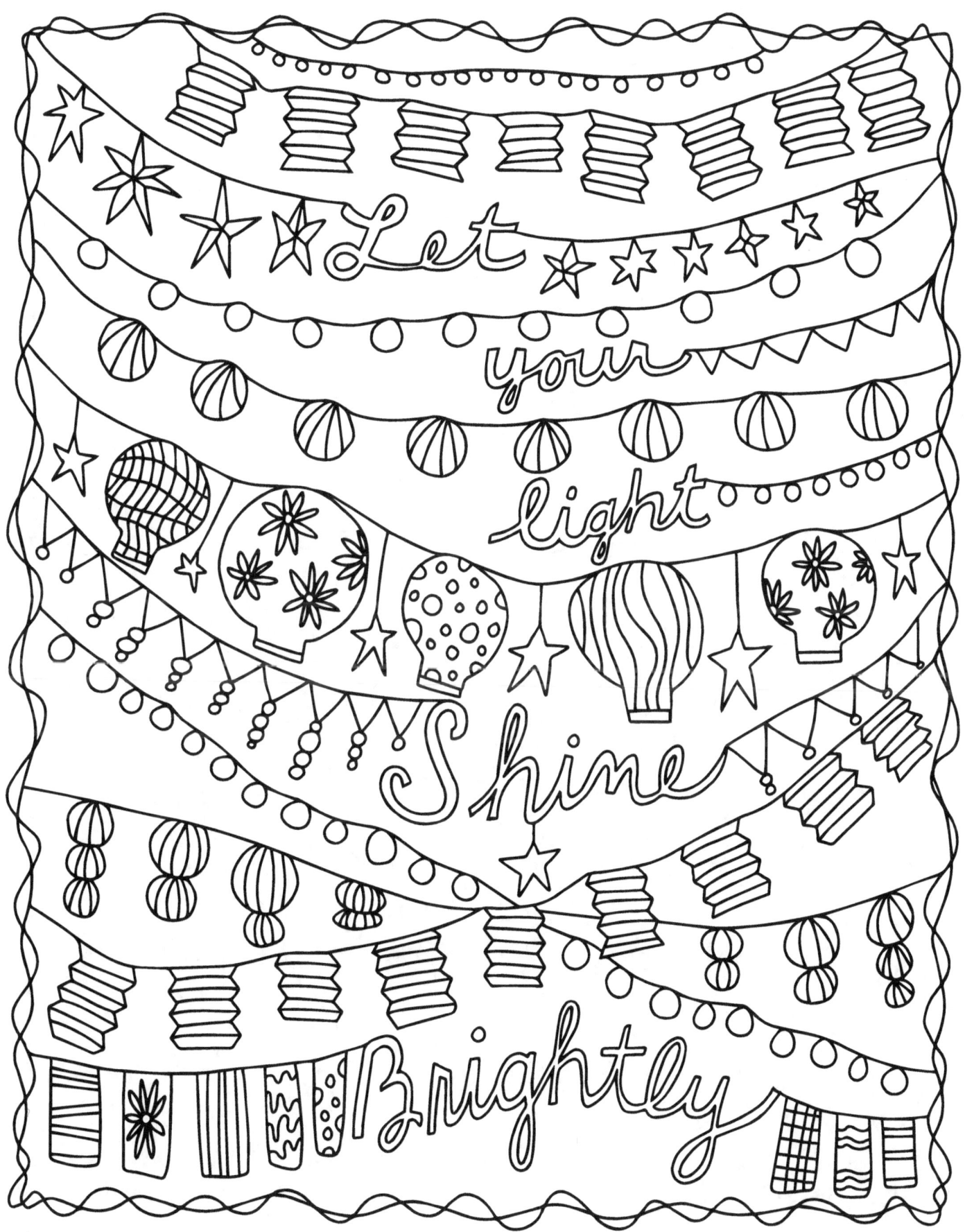

How can you share your gifts with the world?

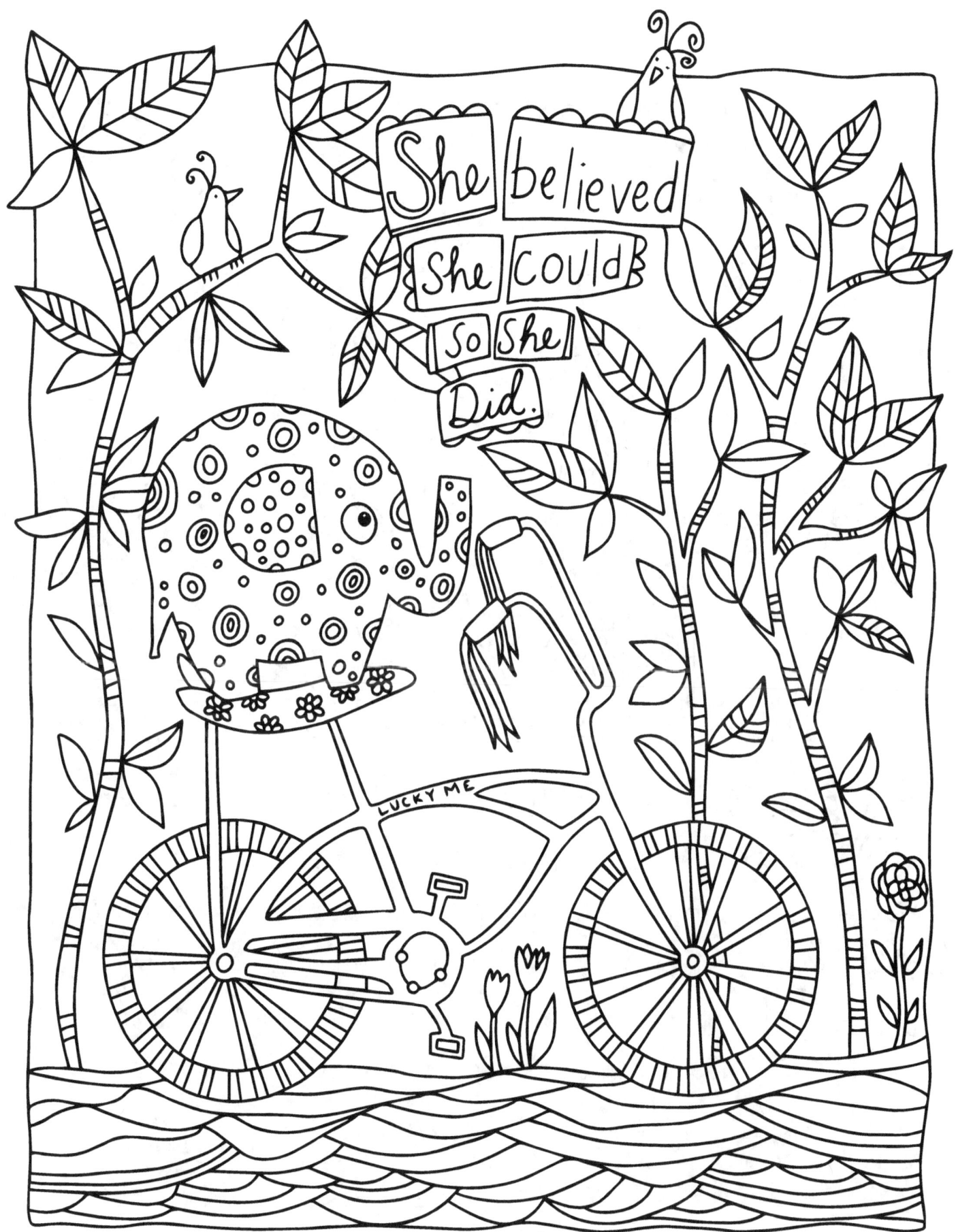

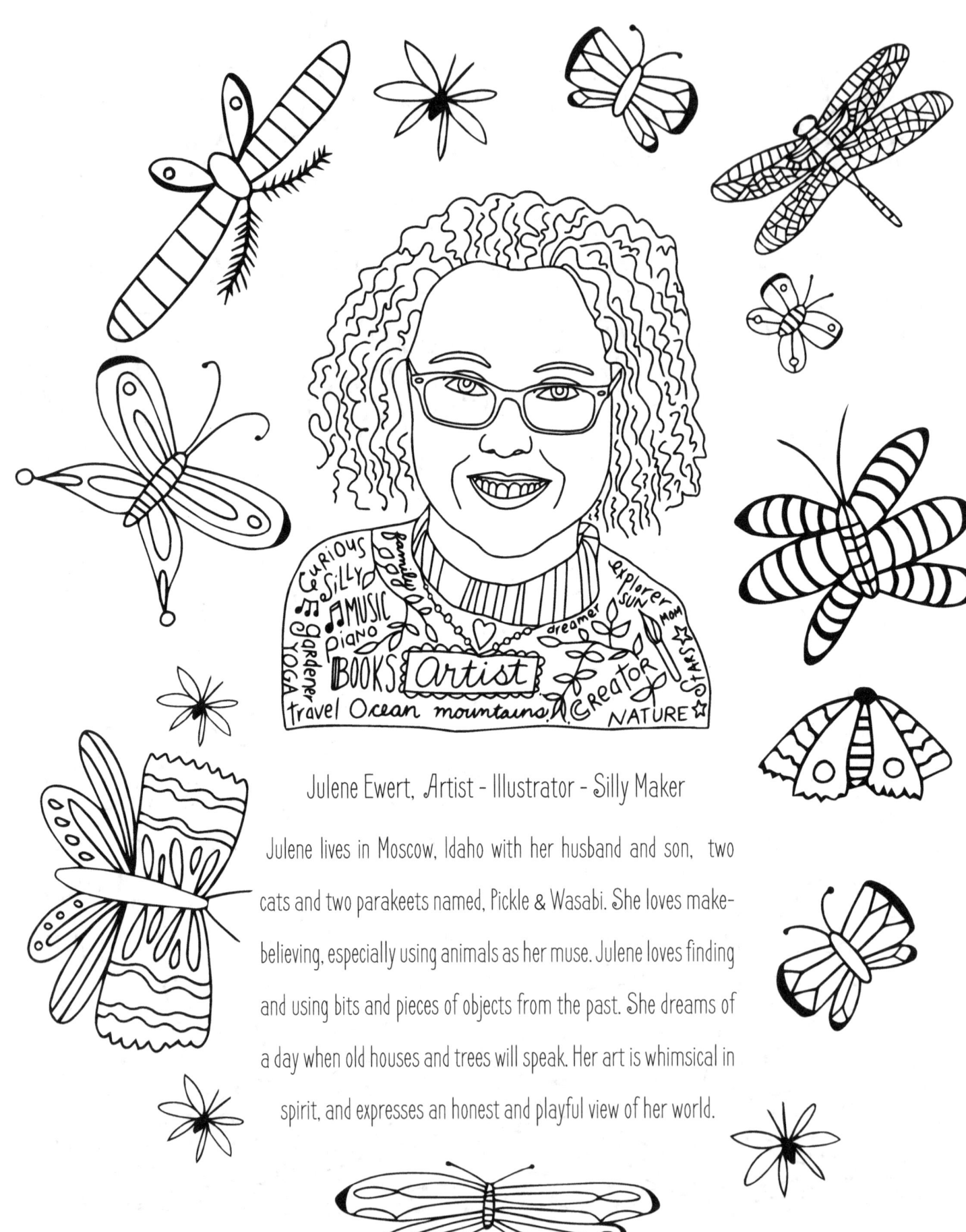

Julene Ewert, Artist - Illustrator - Silly Maker

Julene lives in Moscow, Idaho with her husband and son, two cats and two parakeets named, Pickle & Wasabi. She loves make-believing, especially using animals as her muse. Julene loves finding and using bits and pieces of objects from the past. She dreams of a day when old houses and trees will speak. Her art is whimsical in spirit, and expresses an honest and playful view of her world.

www.ingramcontent.com/pod-product-compliance
Lightning Source LLC
Chambersburg PA
CBHW062226220526
45471CB00009B/3365